HENRI ROUSSEAU

Dora Vallier

HENRI ROUSSEAU

Harry N. Abrams, Inc. *Publishers* New York

Frontispiece: *Avenue in the Park of Saint-Cloud*, 1908

Photograph credits

The author wishes to thank the following photographers whose work appears in this book: Laniepce, Routhier, Spreng, Rosie Rey, and the firms of Giraudon and Viollet

Library of Congress Catalog Card Number: 62–16467

Copyright in Germany by M. DuMont Schauberg, Cologne
Printed and bound in West Germany

Contents

Preface

Until 1960—fifty years after Rousseau's death—all that was known about the man was biographical legend, while the work seemed to consist merely of some widely scattered, isolated paintings. This book is intended to fill out our knowledge. We have set ourselves the task of reopening "the Rousseau file," gathering together all available documents and other information, and scrutinizing it carefully. Many facts previously overlooked have come to the surface, casting almost wholly new light on Rousseau's career. From Rousseau the man we have gone on to Rousseau the artist, studying his methods of work. Little by little the characteristic features of this strange painter have become comprehensible, and we have discovered the sources for several of his paintings, including *War* and *The Sleeping Gypsy*. We can now recognize pictures Rousseau retouched years after he first finished them. The result of our research is that we can at last follow the evolution of this highly self-contained artist. Analysis of wider information has permitted us to draw up a chronological table of his works.

Thus, this book is a first attempt to present Rousseau's art in historical perspective. Needless to say, our primary concern was to collect all the paintings which can unhesitatingly be attributed to Rousseau and to discard those which, as it appears to us, are not his. It would, however, be improper to claim that we have established the definitive catalogue of his works; unfortunately, there is no rigorous scientific basis for such an undertaking. Too much of Rousseau's life and painting remains in shadow. Our ambition has been limited to casting as much light as possible on Rousseau's approach to art, and to drawing a line of demarcation between clearly authentic and clearly counterfeit works. Our selection of illustrations has been dictated by these considerations.

We wish to express special thanks to Mme Sonia Delaunay, M. Tristan Tzara, and M. Michel Bignou for the documents they kindly put at our disposal—some of which are published here for the first time—as well as to M. Henri Bing-Bodmer, Mr. Douglas Cooper, and Mlle Anne-Marie Uhde for valuable suggestions which facilitated our task.   D. V.

Life

Henri Rousseau, known as the Douanier, died in 1910 at the age of sixty-six. Museums and important collectors all over the world have long been vying with one another to possess his works. His place in the history of art is uncontested. And yet, just who was this humble employee of the Paris municipal toll-collecting service who retired at the age of forty in order to devote himself to painting? And what were the sources of his highly original art? It is ironic that in this age of "scientific" art history, all we have in the way of answers to these questions about a recent major figure in modern painting is a legend. Like the Middle Ages which in its thirst for faith seized upon the lives of the martyrs and blew them up to legendary proportions, so, too, the twentieth century, in its mounting passion for all things aesthetic, has in the case of the Douanier Rousseau preferred myth to historical fact. Ever since his first appearance on the historical scene the Douanier has been moving farther away from us, not closer. It is surely time to reverse the trend. Our purpose here is to take a closer look at his life and works and to try to grasp what really went on in that studio in the Rue Perrel—which still exists—in Paris when it was occupied by a poor and poorly educated man who had dedicated his life to painting—according to the legend, sleeping in his clothes "so as to save time."

We can read every published statement by persons who actually knew the Douanier Rousseau and follow up their eyewitness accounts with others as yet not committed to paper, and still find it impossible to reconstruct his personality. The man himself eludes us—and more than that, he will always elude us. What his contemporaries remember of him seems fragmentary, desultory, and full of contradictions. It is impossible to decide whom to believe, whom to disbelieve. For one thing, the most factual accounts of him that we possess concern only the last years of his life—though he had exhibited at the Salon des Indépendants for twenty-five years. What was his life like during those years? And what was it before, when he was with the toll-collecting service at the gates of Paris? For that matter, what had he been as a young man in the provinces, before he went to Paris?

The strange world revealed by his painting raises all these questions. Rousseau's contemporaries tried to answer them, but nearly all of their accounts were published after his death, when he was no longer around to confirm or deny them. For my part, I wonder whether he would have bothered to do either. The case of Rousseau is very complex, with many facets pointing in several directions at once. It is only thanks to his posthumous fame that any biographical data has been checked, let alone corrected. The documents discovered do not take us very far, but today we do possess much more precise information about his life than did his contemporaries. On the other hand, his contemporaries did have the advantage over us of having known and talked with him. And since we propose here to outline Rousseau's life as completely as possible, it seems that the best method to follow is the purely documentary one, filling it out with accounts by his contemporaries when they help bring him to life.

The following is Henri-Julien Rousseau's birth certificate:

"In the year one thousand eight hundred and forty-four, May twenty-first, at three o'clock in the afternoon, there appeared before us in our capacity as municipal councillor, in the absence of the mayor and his assistants, performing the duties of the civil register officer at Laval, chief town in the département of Mayenne, Julien Rousseau, tinsmith, born at Laval 5 May, 1808, residing here in the Place Hardy, who presented to us a male infant born yesterday at one o'clock in the house occupied by himself and by Eléonore Guyard, his wife, born at Laval on 15 August, 1819, and there married in 1837, to which infant he stated were given the names Henri Julien Félix.

"The above-mentioned declaration and presentation, made in the presence of Pierre Soutif, hatmaker, aged 30, and Francis Leroy, tailor, aged 49, residing at Laval, were signed after having been read by the father, the witnesses, and ourself."

Thus, Henri Rousseau was born into that class of independent provincial artisans which survives century after century as if the world never changed. Julien Rousseau was a tinsmith just as his father Julien-Gervais had been, the archives inform us. He gave his son the same Christian name, no doubt expecting him to go right on being a tinsmith in Laval, friend in turn to his neighbors, the hatmaker and the tailor. Henri-Julien was the first son born to his parents. He had three older sisters, Marie, Eléonore, and Henriette, and was to have one younger brother, Jules. The family lived in the Place Hardy where the Cathedral and the Porte Beucheresse stand, the latter a relic of the town's fifteenth-century fortifications. This is the heart of the old town, situated just under the castle. However, the painter's stories in later life never touched on his childhood memories of Laval; his contemporaries would not have failed to mention them, if there had been any, but there is not the slightest reference to them in their published writings. Close scrutiny of the municipal archives of Laval was required to turn up the few scanty facts we have. In 1937 Maximilien Gauthier was able to report that "throughout the nineteenth century, possibly thanks to some sale of national property by the government, the Rousseau family lived in the Porte Beucheresse." Thus, it was in one of the towers of the old city gate that the Douanier Rousseau seems to have come into the world. His father's shop, according to Gauthier, was still extant when he wrote, and fronted on the Place Hardy. According to Trohel, it was situated on the ground floor of a little house near the Porte Beucheresse that was demolished in 1890 when the street was widened. Trohel, a local archivist who, as early as 1928 had studied the municipal register, was the first to give us some details (supplemented since) on the artist's ancestors.

It would seem that his origins were less humble on his mother's side than on his father's. The mother's family, too, had roots in the region, but belonged to another social stratum. The artist's maternal grandfather was one Captain Jean-Baptiste Guyard, who was killed at Bône in 1833, during the conquest of Algeria, and his great-grandfather was Jean-Pierre Guyard, the infantry colonel who "fought in all the Napoleonic campaigns, was commander of the fortress of Sélestat, member of the Légion d'honneur and Chevalier in the order of Saint-Louis." As might be expected, so glorious a past had not been utterly forgotten. As the artist's granddaughter, Mme Jeanne Bernard, recalled (in a memoir published in 1947), her uncle Jules—the artist's younger brother whom she knew well, for like him she lived in Angers—owned some "superb paintings": the portraits of Julien Rousseau, the artist's father, of his wife, and of their ancestors. From these portraits it is possible to get some idea of the kind of life the Rousseaus led, but only by inference, without confirmation by any other document. Were the artist's parents closer to the bourgeoisie than to the small artisan class? It is certain that they came from different backgrounds, but—this curious detail is supplied by the municipal archives—before their marriage the father and mother had both lived in the same street, the Rue des Serruriers, back of the Porte Beucheresse. Their union was the very archetype o fall such among persons who are born, live, and die within the same narrow horizons, unaware of worlds elsewhere. We can guess what their life must have been, and that of their eldest son Henri, so long as he remained in Laval. It is only a step from the Rue des Serruriers to the Place Hardy—and only another step from there to the Lycée of Laval. And yet, not until recently, when Henri Certigny published the results of his research, has anything been known about this period of the Douanier's life.

Henri Rousseau was scarcely seven years old when the family dwelling had to be sold to pay off the debts his father had incurred. When his hardware shop had been disposed of as well, Julien Rousseau became a wine salesman and settled his family at Avesnières and a short time later at Couptrain (both small towns near Laval), where he went into another business. As a result, instead of being a day pupil at the Lycée of Laval, Henri became a boarder. "He seems to have left this school in 1860, which is the year his name ceases to appear on the prize list," Certigny writes. "Thus Rousseau attended school for at least eleven years. An average student, he passed his exams and won a few prizes, including one in vocal music, and one in drawing."

In these recently unearthed documents we begin to catch a glimpse of the painter-to-be, who would always keep up his love of music. Thanks to them we are also made acquainted with a more surprising bit of information, which helps account for the artist's habit of never referring to his early life. At the age of nineteen he was arrested for theft and embezzlement and sentenced to one month's imprisonment. It was in connection with this affair that he enlisted in the army.

In 1863, Henri Rousseau was working for an attorney in the town of Angers. Together with two other young men he perpetrated some petty thefts which were eventually discovered. His crimes had consisted of appropriating ten francs which his employer had given him for other purposes, of stealing postage stamps to the amount of one franc, and of keeping five francs which one of his fellow delinquents had given him for safekeeping. He might never have been found out, were it not for the fact that his friends had made off with rather larger sums of money, taken from Rousseau's employer, among other victims. A complaint was lodged against Henri Rousseau and his friends. It was then that Rousseau, in order to save his honor and escape the reformatory, signed up for a seven-year enlistment—this was the period of military service at the time. But since he had been charged with the crime before enlisting, he was tried and sentenced to one month of imprisonment. At his trial he wore the military uniform and was taken directly from the court to prison. From there he was sent to a penitentiary for a few days, and finally to the Nantes prison where he served his sentence. A reluctant soldier at best, he managed to get out of the army after four years—taking advantage of a decree authorizing unlimited leave for men who were the sole support of widowed mothers. He was twenty-four when he completed his active service.

The next year, 1869, we find Henri Rousseau married and living in Paris at 15 rue Rousselet. His army record contains the following description: "Height 1 m 65 cm [5′ 5″]. Face oval. Forehead round. Eyes black. Nose average. Mouth medium. Chin round. Hair and eyebrows dark brown. Special marks: scarred left ear." His wife, Clémence Boitard, was fifteen years of age. She was a native of Saint-Germain-en-Laye, the daughter of a cabinetmaker who had died. The artist's daughter remembered her mother's family as kind, unpretentious people. She also tells us that one of her maternal ancestors had come from Prague and was "related to the lesser nobility."

The last-mentioned detail has caused a good deal of ink to be spilled. Some writers have assumed, quite wrongly, that this ancestor accounts for the mysterious Yadwigha, a Polish or Russian woman painted by the artist and the subject of a poem by him. While it is true, as we shall see later, that "Yadwigha" was his name for a woman with whom he later fell in love, the name itself does not go back to this period, let alone have any connection with his wife's family. It is true that we must rely upon inferences in re-creating what we can of Rousseau's life, but in this case too much has been deduced from very little evidence. In Rousseau's life the bounds of possibility are extremely blurry, and if we are not to lose ourselves in legend, we must keep strictly to such few facts as we possess.

Thus we know that Rousseau worked as a process server's clerk some time after he was married, but only for a few months. Thanks to his wife's cousin he was able to find employment in the Paris octroi—that branch of the Paris municipal services concerned with collecting tolls at the gates of the city on merchandise brought into it. Of course, we wonder why he made this change. Was he bored by the indoor life of a clerk, "scribbling away all day," as some of his biographers maintain? Or did he quit his job with the process server because, as his granddaughter believes, he "was too kindhearted to seize and impound the worldly goods of poor people"? Possibly his was simply the case of a man with no definite ambitions, drifting whichever way opportunity beckoned—a certain apparent indolence indicating that his true desires, still unknown to himself, were as yet unfulfilled. Is not something like this suggested by the way he devoted himself completely to painting after leaving the toll service? The singleness of purpose displayed by the mature man is surely more revealing than anything we can learn about the young Rousseau who, at the age of twenty-five, still had no profession, still had not chosen a career. He did not know that he wanted to be a painter; he could not have known it—painting simply did not exist in the environment of his youth. By temperament Rousseau was anything but a rebel. His true vocation, so long as it remained unformulated, merely acted as a hindrance, keeping him one of those men who remain forever on the margin of whatever occupation they find themselves in. Actually, it was a great piece of luck for him to have found a job with the Paris octroi. Controlling the entry of goods into Paris required neither the expenditure of great energy nor the exercise of much initiative. It was more a modest sinecure than a real job; it left a man free and did not deform his personality. It was his job as a toll collector at the gates of Paris that made it possible for Rousseau eventually to realize where his true vocation lay—and I think it must have been only very slowly, step by step, that he arrived at this self-knowledge.

He had not been married long when he entered the toll service. Every morning he would set out for the check point where he was currently stationed. Judging by certain drawings (fig. 27), he worked sometimes at the Quai d'Auteuil, where goods coming into the city by water were inspected, sometimes at the Pont de Tournelles (according to some biographers), and finally at the

Porte de Vanves. We infer the last from one of his best-known paintings (*colorplate, page 37*). The Porte de Vanves was one of the gates in the old walls of Paris, that had been enlarged under Louis XVI. Here barriers stopped incoming vehicles and persons coming on foot. No goods or foodstuffs were permitted to enter the capital until a municipal toll had been paid—a relic of medieval custom. Such was Rousseau's life for many years, day after day. During this period he had nine children, seven of whom died. His wife died in 1888. Rousseau was now forty-four and, once he had put in twenty years of service with the octroi, would be entitled to retire on a pension. It took him a while to make up his mind, but finally, in 1893, Henri-Julien Rousseau resigned from the Paris municipal customs service. Although posterity has conferred upon him the rank of "Douanier" (customs officer), he was never actually entitled to it, his own rank in the bureaucratic hierarchy being much less exalted.

As we have just seen, there is no more to go on for the first half-century of Rousseau's life than the few bald facts gleaned from French records of vital statistics, supplemented with some very scanty recollections of his daughter Julia (which we know only indirectly from a letter addressed by his granddaughter to the mayor of Laval in 1947). Julia Rousseau lived with her father only until she was about twelve, and as for the granddaughter, she saw the artist only "very rarely, during vacations." "He did not go out of his way to keep in touch with his relatives in Angers," she says. Nor does she conceal the fact that his relatives did not understand him at all. "In our family, the word 'artist' was synonymous with 'perdition.'" Though the letter was never intended as a piece of serious documentation, it has become the precious source of such facts as we possess about the painter's relations with his family. If Rousseau was as sentimental a man as the later years of his life suggest, he must have suffered a great deal from the hostility of his family. Already a widower, he cut himself off still further from his familiar world when he retired to devote himself to painting. That he was a doting grandfather we know from the portrait he painted of his first grandchild in 1890 and exhibited at the Salon des Indépendants. Twenty years later, in a letter in which he bemoans his fate, he speaks of having lost six children, whereas actually seven of his children died at an early age. A mistake? A slip of memory? Whatever it was, it is significant, for it underlines a change which had taken place in Rousseau's character. The artist had now won the upper hand over the aging father with a tendency to brood over the past. Painting now absorbed him entirely, became the core of his existence. It was painting itself that changed the outlook of this petty customs inspector. Because he was a self-taught artist, Henri Rousseau never did acquire the fully emancipated spirit of a painter, but we have only to look at the photograph of the artist, holding a palette, wearing a velvet coat and a Rembrandt-type hat, to grasp what a distance separated Rousseau the artist from Rousseau the minor municipal employee. The contrast is a staggering one—almost a case of imposture. It is no wonder that Rousseau felt estranged from his own past to the point where he forgot it altogether or began to look at it with different eyes. Apollinaire has a story about how "in 1870 Sergeant Rousseau's presence of mind spared the town of Dreux the horrors of the civil war." He had this from the Douanier himself, who, the poet tells us, "liked to elaborate on the circumstances of this exploit, and his voice had a singularly proud accent when he would relate how he had been acclaimed by the people and his fellow soldiers, all shouting, 'Long live Sergeant Rousseau!'" Actually, he had been demobilized very early in 1870 and never saw combat, though he did pass through the Dreux where his regimental depot was located.

The truth is that the Rousseau whom Apollinaire and his friends knew at the beginning of the century no longer had a past. It was as though he had come into the world at the age of forty. The painter was no longer identified with the ex-municipal employee. The discontinuity is of a type frequently observed in the lives of adventurers (and lies behind their frequent changes of identity), but it is exceptional in the life of a creator. In my opinion, this alone accounts for the peculiar mixture of naïveté and shrewdness which characterized the Douanier's behavior, as it also explains the frequent contradictions we find in accounts by persons who knew him. Could there be any more favorable soil for the growth of legends? When the Douanier reached the stage where he was seeing the same people over and over again, he had to invent some sort of past. Then, a curious phenomenon occurred: his painting provided him with the raw materials for a past. Since he excelled in exotic landscapes, his obscure years of military service became a fabulous journey to Mexico. We know today that Rousseau was a member of the 51st Regiment, stationed at Angers—and we know that this regiment did supply reinforcements for the ill-fated expedition to Mexico. But Henri Certigny's researches have recently established that Rousseau enlisted one year after these reinforcements left. At the very most, he may have talked to survivors of the expedition when they got back to Angers in 1867. (A painting, now lost, entitled *The Last Man of the 51st*, which Rousseau exhibited in 1893, would suggest this.) However, his contemporaries were persuaded to believe that Rousseau had personally taken part in Maximilian II's expedition. "When questioned about this period of his life," Apollinaire wrote in 1913, "he seemed to remember only the fruits he had seen there, which the soldiers were forbidden to eat. But his eyes had preserved other memories: tropical forests, monkeys, and strange flowers...."

The dates of his military service and the Mexican war do coincide more or less exactly, and the Douanier's personal reticence combined with his need to provide some explanation for his strange art did the rest. Nonetheless, in the artist's lifetime, Arsène Alexandre published an interview in which he stated that the Douanier acknowledged that "he never traveled farther than the hothouses in the Jardin des Plantes." It is a case where truth is stranger than fiction. Everyone who knew the Douanier believed the legend of his journey to Mexico, and their writings induced others to believe it for many years to come—everyone, that is, except one woman, Roch Grey. An occasional painter and poet, she was primarily a gifted dilettante. Rich, extravagant, and full of sympathy for the Douanier, she was one of the first persons to buy his paintings. She was very clear on this point: "Rousseau used to stand frozen in boundless admiration in front of the hothouses at the Jardin des Plantes in Paris." Thus, she was the only one of his friends who glimpsed the truth. As for the painter himself, he neither confirmed nor denied the legend. All accounts by his contemporaries are unanimous on this score: he never spoke about his past. To Wilhelm Uhde, his first biographer, he said that "his mother was devout, and considering the modesty of her resources, she spent more than she should have on cakes to which she treated members of the clergy." Similarly, he mentioned the years he had spent in the municipal customs service only in connection with ghost stories he liked to tell, and in which—his contemporaries inform us—he firmly believed. But did he really believe in them? The question will come up again as we confront two distinct images of the Douanier—the one he affected or pretended to affect among Parisian intellectuals and avant-garde artists in the last years of his life, and the very different one he evoked within his own milieu. Here, we have tried merely to indicate the bearing of the Douanier's years of obscurity upon his painting—that other identity which fed his legend. In retracing his past, our primary aim is to set aside the latter, in order to focus upon the crucial years when the humble municipal employee first sat down before his easel and, oblivious of the world around him, began to paint.

1   Rousseau, about 1907, in his studio in the Rue Perrel. The paintings seen are *Scouts Attacked by a Tiger*, *Unpleasant Surprise*, and *Country Wedding*

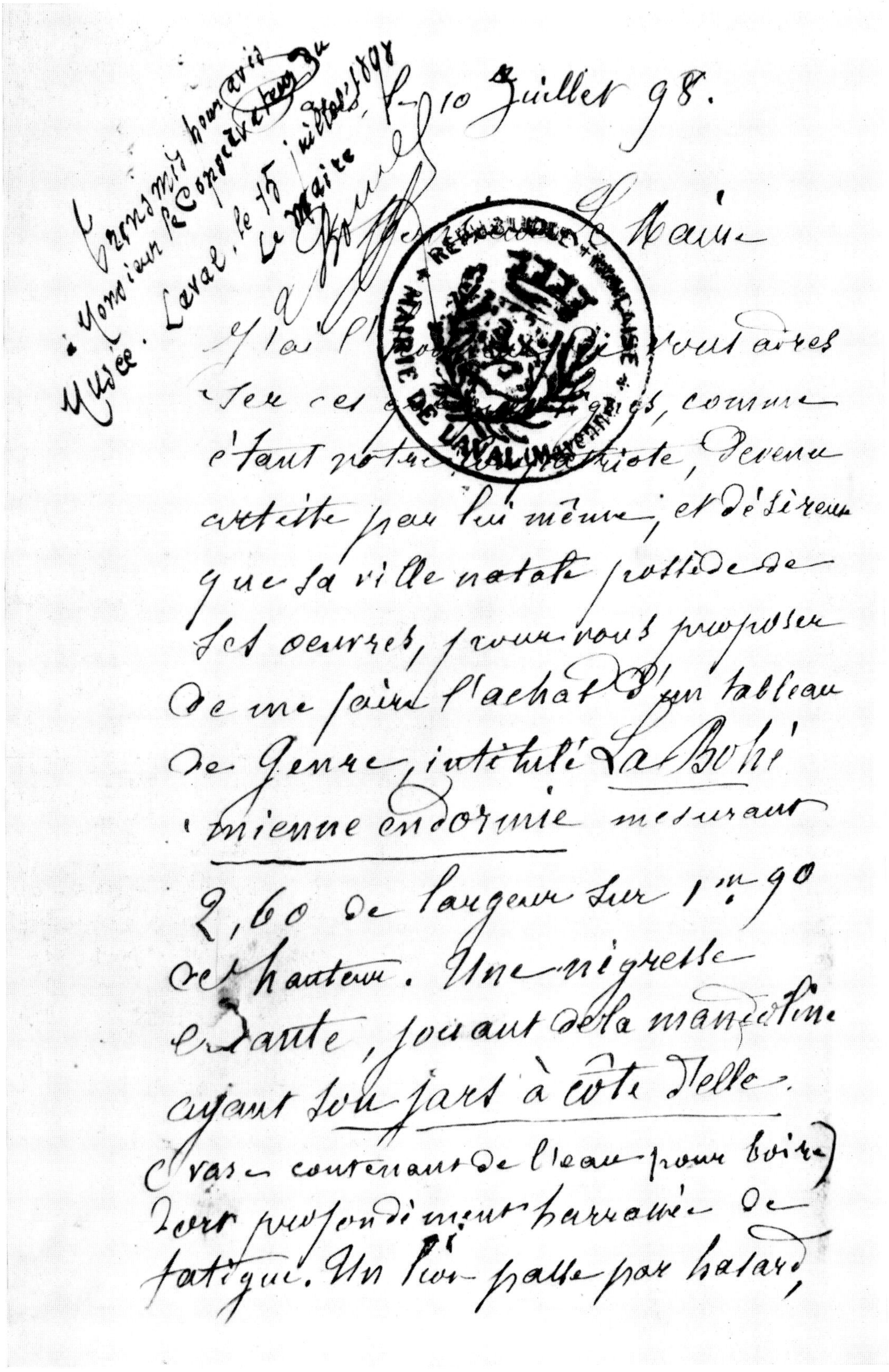

Transmis pour avis à Monsieur le Conservateur du Musée. Laval, le 15 juillet 1898, Le Maire

le 10 Juillet 98.

Monsieur le Maire

J'ai l'honneur de vous adresser ces quelques lignes, comme étant votre compatriote, devenu artiste par lui même, et désireux que sa ville natale possède de ses oeuvres, pour vous proposer de me faire l'achat d'un tableau de genre, intitulé La Bohémienne endormie mesurant 2,60 de largeur sur 1m90 de hauteur. Une négresse errante, jouant de la mandoline ayant son jars à côté d'elle. (vase contenant de l'eau pour boire) dort profondément harrassée de fatigue. Un lion passe par hasard,

RÉPUBLIQUE FRANÇAISE · MAIRIE DE LAVAL (Mayenne)

2 + 3 Rousseau's letter to the mayor of Laval, asking him to purchase *The Sleeping Gypsy*

la plaine, et ne la dévore pas. Bien
un effet de lune, très poétique.
La Scène se passe dans un désert
complètement aride. La Bohémienne est vêtue à l'orientale.

Je vous demande de 2000 à
1800 francs, prix que je
serai heureux que la Ville de
Laval ait un souvenir de
l'un de ses enfants.

Dans l'Espoir, que
mon offre sera accepté avec
faveur, agréez, Monsieur
Le Maire, l'Assurance de
ma Considération distinguée.

Henri Rousseau
artiste peintre

3 rue Vercingétorix.
Paris.

4 Rousseau's calling
   card in 1898–1900,
   when he lived in the
   Rue Vercingétorix

5 Rousseau as a young man

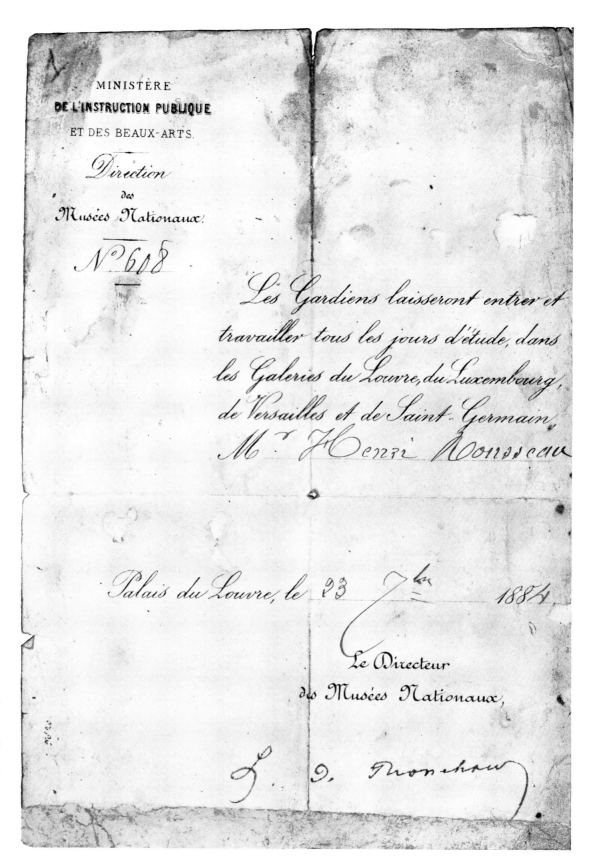

MINISTÈRE
DE L'INSTRUCTION PUBLIQUE
ET DES BEAUX-ARTS.

Direction
des
Musées Nationaux.

Nº 608

Les Gardiens laisseront entrer et travailler tous les jours d'étude, dans les Galeries du Louvre, du Luxembourg, de Versailles et de Saint-Germain, Mr Henri Rousseau

Palais du Louvre, le 23 7bre 1884.

Le Directeur
des Musées Nationaux,

L. D. Tronchew

6 Self-portrait in ink, drawn by Rousseau from the photograph at left. In 1895 Rousseau took this self-portrait and a brief autobiography to the publisher Girard-Coutances, for a volume which was never published. The drawing is at present in the Santamarina collection, Buenos-Aires

7 Rousseau's permit to copy pictures in the national museums, dated September 23, 1884

2. Événement.

ni de la *Danse italienne*, ni de deux ou trois autres ouvrages que nous recommandons aux amis de la gaieté.

Presse

Je suis porté
pour une
spéciale de
2me classe — recommandé par
nos amis le règlement
été clé meux
il a fallu un autre
Ministre de l'
Instruction pu-
blique.

Vie Moderne

Je fus inscrit
pour celle
ni d'ailleurs
d'avoir que
Revue des Beaux
Arts.

Je recommande aux curieux de tourner à gauche en entrant et de s'arrêter devant un tableau portant le nº 289, et intitulé *la Danse italienne*. C'est évidemment l'œuvre d'un enfant de dix ans, qui a voulu dessiner des « bonshommes ». Il faut aussi conclure que ledit enfant ne sait point observer; c'est son imagination qui a fait tous les frais de sa peinture. Il y a là des personnages en carton colorié; c'est un avantage pour l'artiste, puisqu'ainsi ils peuvent prendre des attitudes absolument interdites à tout être humain.

Pendant que je contemple cette étonnante composition, un monsieur, sans doute encouragé par le sourire qui s'épanouit sur ma physionomie, me demande mon crayon. Il désire copier, à titre de curiosité, les vers gravés sur le cadre du tableau. Je me garderai bien d'en faire autant, ils sont du peintre; et si on ne le savait pas, on le devinerait en les lisant!

Ces deux toiles
Danse italienne et
Coucher de Soleil
furent exposées au
Salon. L'une fut
crevée d'un coup de
canif, puis l'on me
fourra pour une
récompense ce qui
fit que je les réexposai
au groupe des dessi-
qui eut lieu au ni...

... que vous... Ceci s'adresse à l'éminent paysagiste Rousseau, dont les toiles ressemblent au gribouillis qui fit les délices de notre sixième année, lorsqu'une boîte de couleurs sans poison nous fut confiée par une mère indulgente, avec nos doigts pour pinceaux et notre langue pour palette. J'ai passé une heure devant ces chefs d'œuvre, examinant les têtes des visiteurs. Pas un qui n'ait ri aux larmes. Heureux Rousseau!

Le publia le Radical qui me remarqua

Les chinoiseries de M. *Rousseau* sont trop primitives pour qu'on s'y arrête longtemps. Nous ne sommes pas encore accoutumés à cette sorte d'imagerie, fort amusante cependant.

Faire des démarches à ce sujet.

9   Waltz by Rousseau, published in 1904. Named after his first wife, it was probably composed before his second marriage in 1899

La Vengeance d'une Orpheline Russe

Drame en 5 Actes et 19 Tableaux (Inédit)

de Mme Barkowsky et Mr Henri Rousseau.

Personnages.

Dames		Hommes	
Mlle Sophie	18 ans Russe	Henri 27 ans Employé de banque à St Pétersbourg allemand
Mme Yadwigha tante russe		Edouard 24 ans Etudiant d°
Mlle Nina	21 ans d°	Le Général Prosquer 76 ans Français
Mme Jeannitta	45 ans d°	Gaston officier de marine russe 28 ans
Mlle Marie domestique 55 ans		Un vieux soldat de la République
Mme Maîtresse d'hôtel 50 ans Française		Gros Pierre 50 ans Russe
Mlle Françoise domestique du Général		Le domestique d'Henri 31 ans d°
... 60 ans Française		Le domestique Gaudinet 50 ans
Mlle Anna domestique 45 ans Russe		Un facteur Un gardien de Cimetière
Foedora d° de Nina d°		Un gendarme à cheval

Bourgeois, paysans flamands et russes.

époque 1855

1er Acte.

La Scène représente des environs de St Pétersbourg, plusieurs petits chalets en bois sur une longue allée en face le petit fleuve de la Neerva. La Maison de Madame Yadwigha est composée de 4 pièces et d'un jardin. Costumes russes (Epoque 58). Madame Yadwigha lit dans le jardin Sophie brode.

La Domestique Anna d'un air navré! Oh! Mesdames, mes bonnes maîtresses, un malheur nous est arrivé. Ce n'est pas qu'il soit bien grand ce malheur, mais ça vous fera bien du chagrin tout de même à toutes les deux. Not' joli canari n'est plus dans sa cage, il s'est envolé oui envolé, j'en' savons point où ma fé. à moins qu'il n'ait été dévoré par un chat, ô pauvre p'tite bête. Ce qu'il y a de certain

HENRI ROUSSEAU. — Le lion, ayant faim, se jette sur l'antilope.

Ancien douanier en retraite, M. Henri Rousseau, auquel les Salons des Indépendants firent fête autrefois pour sa·naiveté miraculeuse et sa gaucherie non apprise, a été accueilli avec un pieux respect au Salon d'automne, où la toile reproduite ici occupe une place d'honneur.

C'est une miniature persane agrandie, transformée en un énorme décor, non dépourvu d'ailleurs de mérité...

THIÉBAULT-SISSON, *le Temps*.

M. Rousseau a la mentalité rigide des mosaistes byzantins, des tapissiers de Bayeux ; il est dommage que sa technique ne soit pas égale à sa candeur. Sa fresque n'est pas du tout indifférente : je concède que l'antilope du premier plan s'adorne à tort d'un museau de brochet ; mais le soleil rouge et l'oiseau apparu parmi les feuillages témoignent d'une rare ingéniosité décorative.

LOUIS VAUXCELLES, *Gil Blas*.

11   In 1905, *L'Illustration* reproduced this painting by Rousseau with excerpts from reviews by the most famous contemporary critics. This was the only reproduction published during his lifetime

12 Rousseau in 1906, in front of *Merry Jesters*

13 Rousseau in 1910, at work on *Exotic Land-scape*

14 Program of one of the "family and musical evenings" Rousseau gave in his studio in the Rue Perrel. He drew these programs himself and had them hectographed

15 A gathering at Rousseau's, with the artist seated at the left. The photograph was once owned by Rousseau

16 Photograph of *The Muse Inspiring the Poet* (Apollinaire and Marie Laurencin). Photograph formerly owned by Rousseau. Toward the end of his career, he systematically had his works photographed. This one, by the photographer Van Echelt, is still on its original "floral" mount

17 Rousseau in 1909. Seen behind him are the *Portrait of Joseph Brummer*, and (unfinished) *The Muse Inspiring the Poet*, which clearly shows how Rousseau worked; the background is completed, while the figures are barely sketched in

18 Page from Rousseau's account book, listing his sales to Vollard

Earliest Paintings

In trying to reconstruct Rousseau's life at the moment he began to paint, we must once again have recourse to statements about him dating from a much later period. Furthermore, these statements must be scrutinized closely, and the circumstances under which they were made taken into account—the more so because they were very special circumstances. The documents we refer to are letters Henri Rousseau addressed to the investigating magistrate from the prison of La Santé. (The episode leading to his imprisonment will be discussed later.) These letters date from 1907, but they were not made public until 1953. One of them, obviously written to arouse the magistrate's sympathy, contains a revealing passage. Referring to the period right after his first wife's death, Rousseau mentioned the trip he made taking his daughter to his brother's home, and adds: "I came back to Paris very dejected and went back to my job. I found myself alone. There was a great void—most of all I missed those two big eyes." This, then, was the atmosphere in which Rousseau's thoughts turned to painting—a succession of bleak and lonely days. In his "great void," whatever he turned to would have to be all or nothing—and we know it soon became all. It would have to make up to him for twenty years of happiness, now come to an end. On this score Rousseau's statements are emphatic: his marriage had been a very happy one. Even allowing for the fact that time lends enhancement to the past, and for the fact that Rousseau, as we shall see, was a sentimental man, other passages in the same letter are eloquent enough: "Married for the first time to a woman I adored ... My poor wife left this earth...after twenty years of a pure and sacred union in which we lived only for each other—as even our parents used to say—and in this way made each other happy. Ah, yes, those twenty years were happy ones...." In short, I am inclined to believe that it was this misfortune which made Rousseau aware of his vocation and strengthened his resolve to devote himself to painting.

It is often asked whether Rousseau had not been painting for a long time before any of his works were exhibited. The mastery displayed in his early works (for instance, *Carnival Evening*, figure 35) would suggest this. And yet I find it hard to believe. From one of his letters we learn that his wife was a consumptive—she may have transmitted the disease to her children, and this would account for their successive deaths. Then comes an admission which we feel to be true: "... and so I plucked up my courage, and on my days off, after strenuous twenty-four-hour tours of duty, I pitched in and helped nurse my patients." His use of the plural is significant. For Rousseau was a kindhearted man—on this point all testimonies agree. And even if they did not, the sentence that follows the one just quoted would suffice: "Fortunately I loved all who were close to me, and for good reasons, so it is no wonder that I behaved blamelessly, never going to cafés or cabarets." These are the words of a devoted family man whose happiness lies in his very devotion, and whose life could not have been an easy one. Even if, during those years, Rousseau already did some drawing or even painting, his work could not possibly have been continuous or systematic, and could never account for the mastery of his early paintings. He was in no position to find the time that such painting requires. The secret of his sudden mastery as a painter must be sought in a thorough study of his pictorial vision; the few biographical details we have just cited are useful only in so far as we focus on the works. Rousseau's painting alone can provide the answer to our question.

Whereas Rousseau had little time for creative work during his years as husband and father, one biographical detail discloses the moment at which painting began to absorb him entirely. This was when he took his daughter, then approximately twelve, to his brother's home in Angers—after which he saw her only rarely, during vacations. The question has given rise to some controversy. Wilhelm Uhde, Rousseau's first biographer, relates that "ignorant of life as he was, Rousseau led a bachelor's existence in the presence of his daughter with such a lack of restraint that the child was taken away from him and placed in another home." On the other hand, Rousseau explains in one of his letters: "After my wife died, the doctor advised my daughter as well as myself to live in the country. I was able to stay a few days with my family and, at the doctor's urging, I left my daughter with them." This is a very different version, and a very plausible one. But apart from accuracy, the essential point is that his separation from his daughter, whatever its motives, was a permanent one. She never lived with her father again. Paternal devotion proved less strong than the appeal of painting. Such were the beginnings of Henri Rousseau's career as a painter.

Later, when he had become a recognized artist in his own eyes, he embroidered on his beginnings. In 1895, in an account of his life which he hoped to see published, he wrote: "Compelled at first by his parents' lack of means to follow a career quite different from that to which his artistic tastes called him, it was not until 1885 that he made his debut in Art after many disappointments and without any master but nature and some advice from Gérôme and Clément." In a letter dating from 1907 he goes back to the same subject: "I was nearly forty when I made my debut in the Arts. I was encouraged by such famous painters as M. Gérôme, Cabanel, Ralli, Valton, Bouguereau, etc. Monsieur Fallières in person, who is today President of the French Republic and was at the time Minister of Public Education, was asked by the late artist Clément, a friend of his, to help and encourage me. Monsieur Clément was Director of Fine Arts in the Ecole de Lyon and had been my neighbor at 135 rue de Sèvres where I lived for twenty years." In another letter, written a few days later, on

Myself: Portrait-Landscape, 1890.

December 19, 1907, he again refers to Clément: "Had my parents known that I was gifted for painting, as they were told by the late Clément who made the portrait of Paul Arène and who was Director of the School of Fine Arts of Lyon, and who was my neighbor at 135 rue de Sèvres, I should be the greatest and richest painter in France today."

Rousseau refers to Clément so often that we cannot help supposing that he was the nucleus around which the legend formed. The elements provided by Rousseau are sufficiently clear. It is possible that the municipal customs inspector made a few drawings one day and at the first opportunity showed them to his neighbor, the famous painter who, from the height of his academic pedestal, encouraged him with the benevolent indulgence that the great usually display toward the humble. It is possible that as a result of this meeting even his own family was for a moment impressed. In any event, it seems certain that some specific recollection of Rousseau's involves Clément. In one of the notebooks in which he pasted newspaper articles about himself, we find a clipping about Clément with the following note in Rousseau's hand: "Note concerning M. Félixe [*sic*] Clément, my teacher-advisor [*sic*], historical painter, grand prix de Rome, from *Mot d'Ordre*, year 1889; it is my duty to continue to respect and be grateful to him, though he is no more, for he always gave me good advice." Did Clément really advise him on more than one occasion? Just when did their meetings take place? Clément was a man of modest origins and for this reason perhaps more accessible than his colleagues. But it would be rash to infer that he ever took much interest in the Douanier. And just when did Rousseau find the leisure to paint? "My superiors at the customs service gave me lighter tasks so as to afford me better opportunities to work," he writes, hinting that he painted while employed by the octroi. Wilhelm Uhde reports this reminiscence by one of Rousseau's former fellow employees: "Rousseau never talked very much ... and didn't joke with his colleagues, but sat by himself painting and drawing." So the question remains: for just how long had he been painting before he began to exhibit?

Unfortunately, there is no way of knowing where fiction begins in the Douanier's stories about himself. It is a fact that he did paint while on the job, thanks to arrangements which are always possible in government offices, the more so because his position involved no responsibilities—at the end of his career as a clerk he was no more than a second-class employee. Until recently it was believed that he had retired in 1885—the year he began to exhibit regularly—and the statements we have just quoted were invoked as evidence for a preparatory period; it was assumed that the Douanier could very easily have begun to paint before 1880. Now that we know he did not retire until 1893, it is obvious that he had been painting for at least nine years. If so, the statements quoted might refer to those nine years, and for my part I think that we must base our conclusions on a crucial statement made on two occasions several years apart. In 1895 Rousseau said that he made "his debut in Art in 1885"; twelve years later he wrote: "I was nearly forty when I made my debut in the Arts." In 1885 Rousseau was indeed "nearly forty"—on this point there can be no doubt whatever. His statement is confirmed, moreover, by one very eloquent fact: in 1884 he obtained a permit to make copies in the galleries of the Louvre, at Versailles, and at Saint-Germain.

While it is thus possible to determine the date when Rousseau began to paint, the greatest possible confusion prevails concerning the date when he began to exhibit his works. Rousseau himself tells us that he exhibited for the first time at the Salon des Champs-Elysées, yet the two titles he mentions, *Italian Dance* and *Sunset*, are not listed in the catalogue. But the Salon des Champs-Elysées was a salon of "official" art, if there ever was one, and it would indeed be surprising if any works by Rousseau had been accepted by the jury. It would seem that the misunderstanding is accounted for by the fact that another Salon was held in the Champs-Elysées in 1884–85, and Rousseau's works may well have been among those exihibited. But since we here touch upon a controversial question which seems to require further clarification, let us look into the matter of Rousseau's early exhibitions somewhat more closely.

At the Salon des Indépendants

In the spring of 1884 posters appeared on the walls of Paris, announcing the foundation of a "Group of Independent Artists" who were proposing to organize a non-jury, no-prize exhibition, to be open to all artists. Several artists whose works had been rejected by the official Salon were behind the project, which received wide discussion. "There was a rush of exhibitors," writes Paul Signac, who was one of the founders of this historic annual Salon which accepted paintings by Seurat, Toulouse-Lautrec, Van Gogh, Cézanne, and—in later years—Bonnard, Matisse, and others.

Rousseau must have seen one of these posters, and in this way happened to become one of the participants in the First Salon des Indépendants, which opened its doors on December 10, 1884, at the Pavillon de la Ville de Paris on the Champs-Elysées. The proceeds were to go to victims of the cholera epidemic. Rousseau wrote in his notebook: "Beginning of 1885, the two canvases *Italian Dance* and *Sunset* were exhibited at the Salon: one was slashed with a penknife, and I was denied compensation, so I exhibited it again with the rejected artists' group, the later exhibition taking place in June."

It is not clear what he means by "compensation," since the novelty of the Salon consisted precisely in the fact that it was open to all artists, without distinction, and that there were no prizes. What we have here is perhaps an instance of Rousseau's characteristic vagueness; he gets his facts mixed up, most often unintentionally—a matter some writers have interpreted as deliberate and willful mystification. As for the canvas exhibited again in June 1885 with the "rejected artists' group," as he says, we know he is referring to the Salon Libre des Beaux-Arts, also called the Salon des Refusés, a rival of the Indépendants, organized on the same principles. The Artistes Indépendants held no exhibition in 1885; the Salon des Refusés was held in a temporary structure put up in the Tuileries. In 1886, the Indépendants won the upper hand; they organized their second Salon, to which the Douanier sent four paintings. From that date until the end of his life he exhibited annually at the Salon des Indépendants. A painter without friends in the art world, a self-taught artist of utter originality, Rousseau was lucky that a non-jury Salon had at last been created.

Thus, Rousseau's amazing career began. He wanted to be a painter, and now he had become one. With public exhibition, he had formally taken the plunge. But what did the decision mean to him? A few lines in a letter he wrote twenty years later preserve, as I read them, a hint of what Rousseau's state of mind must have been at the start of his career: "I was discouraged, I had lost my purest affection [his wife], I was not a materialist, and so my life became that of a philosopher, in love only with nature, whose beauty and grandeur every sincere artist must revere."

For the sake of the exaltation which nature aroused in him, and which he carried over into his paintings, Rousseau had to sacrifice a great deal. "No one will ever know how great were the difficulties he surmounted and the effort of will he displayed to ward off defeat," Roch Grey writes. He was indeed extremely poor. His resources barely sufficed for the most minimal standard of living, and it took twenty years before he began to sell his paintings, apart from a very few commissions—portraits of people in his neighborhood, their children, and shop signs. According to Apollinaire, Rémy de Gourmont once saw the Douanier working on a shop sign right out in the street. Such jobs, however, were rare, and the painter's resources were extremely limited. Legend has it that his laundry woman let him pay her with small canvases, and his grocer as well; there is also the tale of how he attempted, unsuccessfully, to barter a painting for a picture frame. "And to think that old bird used to pay our bills with his own daubs!" an old hardware dealer exclaimed several years after Rousseau's death when his paintings were beginning to fetch impressive prices. "Why, we threw them all out with the other junk long ago—they went to the Flea Market!" It gives us quite an insight into how Rousseau's lonely pursuit of his art was viewed by the people among whom he lived.

Did he suffer from such constant disparagement? I think we have to assume that it had a double-edged effect on him: if it cut him off from the world around him, it must have made him insensitive to judgments passed on him. His mind was on other things. In his scrapbook, next to the earliest newspaper clippings mentioning his name, he wrote: "1886, first exhibition with the Société des Artistes Indépendants, to which I now belong." His pen records a simple, natural pride. Carefully, year after year, he kept on pasting in successive criticisms of his works. Before long, a note of praise appears. Referring to his painting *A Poor Devil*, exhibited in 1887, *Le Mot d'Ordre* said: "A word of encouragement to M. Rousseau, who is not an Impressionist. He is a sincere painter who brings to mind the Primitives. The subject is very naïve! An old man half-clothed in an animal skin, outside his hut in a bleak snowy wood. The title, *A Poor Devil*, is an understatement! I repeat, however, the artist has tried hard, he is sincere, and the work is somehow sympathetic." Marcel Fouquier, critic for the *XIXème siècle*, while praising Rousseau in other connections, fills in the rest of what we know about this lost painting: "Finally, we may mention . . . for its surprising originality, M. Rousseau's *A Poor Devil*," he writes, "showing an old man leaning against a tree in a wood where the ground is covered with snow. The painting is rather dry and harsh, but quite interesting, for it brings to mind the Italian Primitives by its very naïveté. Add a tame lion at the feet of the shivering old man with his fine white beard, and you have one of those miracle-working hermit saints such as Giotto's pupils painted, a Simone Memmi or a Taddeo Gaddi."

How prescient was this critic's insight in 1887! Did his words induce Rousseau to spend time with the Primitives in the Louvre, to study those panels which were so very far from being in vogue at the time? He may very well have done so. Out of pure curiosity he may have gone to see the painters with whom he was being compared. And had his taste been equal to his sensitivity, how much he could have learned from them! The distinguishing mark of the so-called naïve painters, however, is their imperviousness to outside influences, their way of drawing all their strength, and their means of expression as well, from themselves. Rousseau may have read and re-read this excellent review, without deriving from it anything more than encouragement. Such praise confirmed the faith he had in his own gifts—a faith, incidentally, he never concealed, and which grew stronger with time. (Indeed, it led to some grotesque misadventures, to be discussed later.) He may have been similarly affected by the reviews devoted to him the following year on the occasion of the Salon of 1888, where he exhibited five paintings and, for the first time, some drawings. "An interesting series of drawings (H. Rousseau)," we read in *Salon pour tous*; and *Le Cri du peuple* says: "M. Rousseau's trees reveal him as a profound draftsman. I am most particularly anxious to express my complete admiration and sympathy," the critics goes on to say, "for the naïve conscientious works of . . . and those of M. H. Rousseau." This should have taken the sting out of such mocking comments as these: "*A Departure* in the Swiss mountains, the

19   The Toll House at the Porte de Vanves, when Rousseau worked there. Photograph by Atget. Musée Carnavalet, Paris

L'Octroi (The Toll House), about 1890

perspective of which makes the viewer wonder whether he is on his feet or standing on his head" *(Echo du Nord)*; And from *L'Exposition universelle:* "A moment of hilarity is always pleasant: do not deprive yourself of this pleasure by failing to look at M. Rousseau's *Departure*. It is black on white, and it is crude, a real challenge to nature." Today, when we appreciate the quality of Rousseau's blacks, this summary description of a lost painting fairly makes us drool. As for "challenging nature," that may well have annoyed Rousseau—how could anyone say that he, all of whose strength derived from nature, *challenges* it? How wrong can a critic be? Rousseau never doubted himself, however—on the contrary, his self-confidence increased. The following year, the year of the 1889 World's Fair, he was so exalted by everything he saw in Paris that he overflowed. Painting no longer sufficed to contain his need for self-expression, and he began to write. The result was a light comedy in three acts and ten scenes, entitled *A Visit to the 1889 Fair*.

Influence of the Paris World's Fair of 1889

Surprisingly, no biographer of Rousseau has as yet touched on the part played by the World's Fair of 1889 in the artist's life. This is the more surprising because the event was a striking one, with widespread repercussions.

For the ordinary people of Paris, the World's Fair of 1889 was especially memorable—an unprecedented sensation. Rousseau, who was one of these ordinary people (though he had become a painter), derived more than others from it: it increased his confidence in his own approach to art. We can scarcely appreciate today what it meant to find right in Paris, before one's eyes, models and samples of the life, the art, and the sciences of even the most faraway lands—Western progress side by side with fantastic flora and fauna. It was so impressive precisely because it was all scaled down to the vision of the ordinary man, deliberately presented so as to appeal to the masses. Today we have become so used to thinking of the artist as standing out—an exception to or even in opposition to all we think of as "mass culture"—that Rousseau's very different attitude escapes us, rooted in the sensibility of the masses as it was. What impressed the ordinary people of Paris impressed him, too, and influenced his painting. There is a great deal of evidence for this. All the time critics and biographers have been looking for him in the Louvre he was actually over at the Champ de Mars, studying the serious, rather pompous displays at the 1889 World's Fair. Lacking the discrimination which is the fruit of culture and which is sharpened by it, Rousseau possessed the omnivorous curiosity of the auto-didact, and since he was essentially an artist, his imagination was fired by all the new things he saw. Moreover, he recorded them in terms of his own lyrical temperament, so that in the end what he accumulated was a private store of sensations rather than a collection of scientific data. He was no longer the man who, because he had become a painter, merely perceived the existence of a world that was different from his own, but remained remote, closed to all men like him who had not been taught to gain access to it; now he could know everything—everything a painter needs to know.

Swept along like other Parisians by the enormous publicity, he went to the Fair again and again. For the six months it was open, the Fair was the most important event of the day, and to the common people it was the most important event of the century. Since 1889 was the centenary of the French Revolution, the government organized grandiose patriotic and popular festivities, reminiscent of the festivities of 1789. Citizen Henri Rousseau felt at home in this atmosphere. Like hundreds of thousands of other visitors, here he saw electric light for the first time: it made its triumphant entry into everyday life during the Fair, illuminating the fountains and climbing into the sky with the 984-foot metal tower (named Eiffel after its builder) which had been specially constructed for the Fair. However, it was not the nocturnal glitter that most strongly appealed to Rousseau's imagination. At the foot of the Eiffel Tower was assembled a collection of "native villages" representing the peoples, the flora, the fauna, and the characteristic ways of life of five continents. Here it was that Rousseau found "scale models" of the whole world, humanity in microcosm—an approach to reality which influenced several of his paintings and inspired his play.

Close examination of the iconographic repertory of certain of the Douanier's paintings discloses that he was interested in the 1889 World's Fair both as a citizen and as an artist. His episodic comedy, *A Visit to the 1889 Fair*, reflects both interests and reveals the man and his psychology.

Deeply imbued with the ideals of the French Revolution, Rousseau was particularly stirred by the celebrations commemorating it, the apogee of which was the now-forgotten presentation of the *Ode Triomphale* by Augusta Holmès, an impressive popular spectacle involving 1,200 actors, and choruses, and orchestra. Putting on the stage a procession of all occupations—wine growers, farmers, soldiers, sailors, and industrial workers—it symbolized the unity of the French nation under the Third Republic. Inevitably, we recall two of Rousseau's paintings, *The Centenary of Independence (colorplate, page 45)* exhibited in 1892, and *The Carmagnole (fig. 55)*, in which the date "1893" is inscribed on a flag. The painter thus commemorated the hundredth anniversary of the proclamation of the Republic (1792) and the famous revolutionary song and dance of 1793. In both paintings, which are very similar, ordinary people are shown dancing around the Tree of Liberty. At the center hangs the tricolor crossed with the flag of the city of Paris. The presence of the latter flag, painted blue and red, is of itself sufficient to point to the World's Fair, for the colors of the city were displayed a great deal at this time. A few other details are even more directly traceable to the *Ode Triomphale*. I am referring to the strange figures which appear on banners at the right and the left, and which may correspond to the description we have of the spectacle: "On the stage, around the choruses, were flags bearing figures—Wine, Harvest, War, the Sea, Labor, Industry, Engineering, Reason, Love, Youth" *(fig. 56)*.

Finally, the Phrygian (or "Liberty") cap worn by the figures in both paintings is also an accessory taken from the World's Fair. Rousseau is explicit on this score in his play. The scene is laid at the Invalides, at an exhibition devoted to the glorious military exploits of French history (a part of the World's Fair which drew more visitors than any other). The servant girl in this scene exclaims, "It's a big painting, full of people . . . . And their caps are all red! Why is that?" "These are Phrygian caps," she is told. These "liberty caps" of the Revolution soon make their appearance in Rousseau's pictures—even when treating historical subjects, he was above all a painter of feeling. Feelings remained with him in the form of reminiscences until he had succeeded in embodying them in his pictures: the example just cited is very clear. In fact, it suggests that two other paintings had a similar origin. They were exhibited at the Salon des Indépendants in 1893 and have not survived, but we know the titles and the accompanying explanatory notes. It seems obvious that they recalled impressions of the World's Fair. The first, entitled *Freedom*, was provided with a caption saying, "O Freedom, be ever the guide to all who by their work seek to contribute to France's greatness and glory!" The second is the previously mentioned *The Last Man of the 51st*, at the bottom of which was the following caption: "After long battles the regiment was completely decimated; only this poor cripple is left to save the flag under which his elders had won such fame." This was an allusion to the Mexican War. Even though the content may be linked with Rousseau's years of military service, the painting was executed only after he had seen the numerous panels treating military subjects at the Invalides.

Still other paintings by Rousseau are connected with the World's Fair, but less directly. Thus, in *View of the Pont de Grenelle (fig. 57)*, the Statue of Liberty lighting the world which is shown at the right was a gift of the American

Surprised! (Storm in the Forest), 1891

colony to the city of Paris, made in 1889, during the Fair. This was an occasion for one of six special after-dark galas at the Fair, which drew Parisians en masse. It is possible that the Douanier noticed the statue then. However, the statue is not the center of the composition, and its presence merely suggests a date for the painting, as does the fact that the ground is shown covered with snow. Rousseau's views of Paris are never fanciful: they record what he actually saw. Here the snow testifies to the unusually severe winter of 1891.

Finally, it must be kept in mind that the Eiffel Tower—constructed for the World's Fair—occurs frequently in Rousseau's paintings. He treated it as early as 1890, when it had been condemned to destruction, "because it is so ugly."

Rousseau's reactions to the World's Fair so far discussed are the same as those of the masses, and they concern us only to the extent that he transfigured them in art. But there is also an instance which reflects his artistic sensibility, namely, his interest in exotic vegetation. Its role in Rousseau's style is well known; what is less well known is that the World's Fair greatly contributed to it. Rousseau had displayed a taste for the exotic even before 1889; he was familiar with the hothouses and animals at the Jardin des Plantes. In his play, the characters who come to Paris to visit the Fair are also sent to the Jardin des Plantes. At the fair itself, however, he must have been thrilled by the Tonkinese, Senegalese, and Tahitian villages set up there, with natives in exotic costumes strolling about to the accompaniment of their musical instruments. He must also have been impressed by the central garden of the Algerian pavilion, which featured lush African flora, and by the lawn with tropical plants surrounding the Mexican pavilion. Inside the latter were hundreds of animals, both alive and stuffed. The impressions must have been dazzling to the point of confusion, yet they are at the origin of Rousseau's first exotic painting, *Surprised! (Storm in the Forest) (colorplate, page 41)*, dated 1891. Finally, supplementary proof of Rousseau's enthusiasm over the World's Fair is found in the painting entitled *Transatlantic Liner in a Storm (Storm at Sea) (fig. 54)*. A somewhat unexpected work to cite in this connection, still it seems certain that the painter had visited the Panorama which the Compagnie Transatlantique had mounted on pilings in the Seine. On the second floor of that exhibit was a reconstruction of the bridge of the steamship Touraine, and viewed from there the illusion of being at sea was complete. A contemporary description reads: "Thanks to an extremely ingenious arrangement, the traveler is surrounded by the sea on all sides, as far as the eye can see, while, dotted all around are the company's splendid liners." The ship painted by Rousseau is indeed a transatlantic liner with rows of portholes and powerful smokestacks.

All the paintings mentioned above are in different ways connected with the World's Fair, but they were executed in the years immediately after it. Rousseau never painted in a hurry, as we shall see later when we discuss his working habits. But the surge of impressions aroused by the Fair was so strong that it had to be externalized as soon as possible. His play was finished before the Fair closed. It tells us a good deal about Rousseau. The action is that indicated in the title: a visit to the 1889 Fair. The characters, like himself natives of Brittany, serve to project the writer's avid curiosity at several levels, but at the same time he remains detached, dominating and caricaturing the action. The comical effects are never wounding and are cleverly contrived. The play (the manuscript seems to be the first draft) moves at a fast pace. Rousseau must have loved the theater, and in this work turns his love to his advantage. Expressing himself gave him self-confidence. He had long been an anonymous Breton, swallowed up in the capital and dazzled by it. Now he was something different—an artist. He had seen and learned many things. The play is more than a guide to his sources of inspiration (it is the document of a crucial experience, his experience of the World's Fair) which in the life of this self-taught painter were to hold the place more customarily assigned to formal schooling. The play lets us feel very clearly what an enhanced stature he had taken on in his own eyes. In it he views himself calmly and with self-assurance, and draws a self-portrait as unmistakable as a calling card.

Rousseau's Painting from 1890 to 1895

The World's Fair closed in October 1889. In March 1890, Rousseau exhibited a self-portrait at the Salon des Indépendants under the title *Myself: Portrait-Landscape (colorplate, page 31)*. Against the festive background of a ship decked with pennants, Rousseau stands proudly, wearing a beret, palette in one hand, brush in the other. Dressed in black, the white cuff barely visible at the coat sleeve, his impeccable attire conveys the sense of respectability which his contemporaries noticed in him. Here he is the respectable painter. His beard is graying, his expression is intense. Reality is mingled with aspiration here, and the portrait attains a profound truth, which nobody else so much as suspected in 1890, namely, that this man is a great painter.

At the Salon des Indépendants, visitors laughed in front of the self-portrait. The reviewers were ironical. "No doubt because of his excessive modesty," said *XIXème siècle*, "the artist painted himself as a midget, with an oversized head, perhaps overburdened with ideas . . . .You are advised to feel both moved and disarmed. . . ." And the critic on the *Journal des Arts* wrote: "I found it hard to get close to M. Henri Rousseau, whom I shall take the liberty of calling the chief attraction at the Indépendants. M. Rousseau is an innovator. It is he who invented the 'portrait-landscape,' and my advice to him is to take out a patent on his invention, for there are unscrupulous individuals capable of making use of it."

But Rousseau was impervious to irony. His faith in his art was so unshakable that it colored his attitude toward the critics. This is perhaps one of the aspects of his naïveté. He was entirely sincere when he wrote in a letter in 1907: "I am the inventor of the portrait-landscape, and I was mentioned as such in the press." He was convinced that he was merely telling the truth, quoting his critics faithfully. Whenever Rousseau came into contact with the outside world, this was his characteristic spontaneous reaction (and essentially that of every lonely, misunderstood man). He could not follow any but his own ideas. At grips with people and things, he inadvertently provoked situations where nobody lied and nobody told the truth. Rousseau resisted any effort to "unmask" him for the simple reason that he never wore a mask.

Though he was impervious to irony, he was not insensitive to praise. "In all my works Sincerity has been observed," he wrote, capitalizing the word, "and I have always aimed at it in my actions as well as in my work." And who can deny it? If his paintings provoked laughter, were not the same viewers just as blind when they stood in front of the other exhibits at the Indépendants, works signed Van Gogh, Toulouse-Lautrec, Seurat? Stubbornly, Rousseau awaited the day when he would be famous. It must have seemed to him that fame was on its way one day in 1890 when he received the following letter in the form of a poem, addressed to him by an unknown woman:

> *O toi, Henri Rousseau*
> *Fils aîné du génie*
> *Débarass [sic] nous de la coterie*
> *Des Cabanel et des Bouguereau*
> *Grand talent méconnu*
> *Qui vaut mieux que le leur*
> *Mon cœur en toi a reconnu*
> *Celui qui peut faire mon bonheur.*

[Signed]: Une admiratrice qui tremble à la pensée de votre verdict.

> [O thou, Henri Rousseau,
> Eldest son of the genius,
> Rid us of the clique
> Of the Cabanels and Bouguereaus.
> Great misunderstood talent,
> You are better than they are.
> My heart has recognized in you
> The man who can make me happy.

[Signed]: A feminine admirer who trembles at the thought of your verdict.]

The Centenary of Independence, 1892

The letter is written in a beautiful, careful hand, its refinement oddly marred by the strange misspelling, which seems to have been deliberate. Was it a joke? Such an idea would never have occurred to Rousseau. He pasted the poem in his notebook, next to his press clippings. A few pages later we find another poem in the same hand, in the same tone: "O France, you will be proud...." There can be no doubt that Rousseau was touched by it. The unknown woman was the only person who had seen him as he painted himself in *Portrait-Landscape*.

The self-portrait was a real double, a more authentic Rousseau than the man who painted it. Rousseau must have lived a long time with this painting. Let us look at it more closely. Two women's names are inscribed on the palette: Clémence and Joséphine. Clémence was his dead wife. And Joséphine? Joséphine was his second wife's name, but he did not marry her until 1899, nine years after the self-portrait was painted. In fact, her name was painted in later, and it is surprising that the correction has not been noticed before. Rousseau painted out a shorter name, probably his own, and replaced it with Joséphine's. The picture thus records the painter's progress from lonely widowhood to new-found happiness. Note, however, that Clémence's name was not removed—a noble, as well as sentimental, gesture. In 1901, when he became a teacher at the Ecole Philotechnique, he added an academic insignia to the lapel. As Rousseau got ahead in life he saw to it that the self-portrait reflected his status.

The names on the palette had been noticed before this, and the meaning of the academic insignia deciphered, but what makes them especially significant is that they were additions to the picture as originally painted. We can grasp better today the extent to which this work mirrored the painter's existence over more than a decade. The painter kept tabs on his progress.

The *Portrait of Pierre Loti (fig. 48)* dates from the same period and also gives evidence of Rousseau's growing self-assurance. Like Clément and other painters he regarded as his masters, Rousseau wanted to do the portrait of a prominent contemporary. He betrays this in the letter of 1907, mentioned earlier, where he wrote: "The late Clément, who painted the portrait of Paul Arène." The fact that of all Clément's works he chooses to mention this secondary painting is the more significant because the sentence in question falls out of context. What motivated him if it was not a desire to be faithful to the academic tradition, according to which artists were expected to portray famous men?

In May 1891, the newspapers reported that Pierre Loti had been elected a member of the French Academy. I think Loti is one of the few writers Rousseau may actually have read. Loti was well known as a naval officer and a great traveler, and much in his writing would have appealed to Rousseau: the facile exoticism of his early novels *(Le roman d'un spahi, Azyadé)*, his sentimentalism, and the fact that the action of *Mon frère Yves* is laid in Brittany, Rousseau's native province. The former municipal customs clerk had a great respect for institutions, so it would hardly be surprising if he were impressed by the decision of the French Academy. If he was at all familiar with Loti's work, this would have been enough to settle on Pierre Loti as the famous man whose portrait he would paint. Moreover, the second part of the bulletin reporting the election of Loti to the French Academy helps to account for certain features of Rousseau's portrait. "The news of his election," we read, "was telegraphed to Lieutenant Viaud who is at present aboard the *Formidable* off Algiers." Isn't it Algiers we see in the background of the portrait, houses climbing up over the hills? Loti wears a fez, almost certainly an allusion to Islam. As far as I am concerned, I doubt that Rousseau supplied these details on his own: they must have appeared in contemporary drawings. Loti was fond of dressing up in native costumes and striking bizarre poses. A photograph showing him in Turkish dress had been known as early as 1876. Rousseau was probably inspired by a sketch published at the moment when Loti was a focus of public attention, and thus the portrait was probably executed between May 1891, when Loti was elected to the Academy, and April 1892, the date when he was officially installed. It is therefore impossible that the painting exhibited in 1891 under the title *Portrait de M. L.* was Loti's portrait, as has been assumed—for the Salon des Indépendants closed on April 27, a month before the newspapers began to discuss Loti. However, it is rather surprising that the portrait was never exhibited, for it is an "official" work par excellence, very much meant to be seen. Rousseau painted it in the hope of becoming better known by the public. His choice of subject was motivated by his unconscious desire to establish contact with people who knew Loti and could make his own reputation. The portrait was to serve as a link between Henri Rousseau the painter, and persons of influence. Why, then, was the portrait never exhibited? It is interesting to note that someone wrote to the Galerie Charpentier, during an exhibition, stating that the "so-called portrait of Pierre Loti" was actually a portrait of himself, and that he, the writer of the letter, sat for the Père Rousseau wearing a fez. In our view, this statement, though doubtless made in good faith, does not tell the whole story. As we shall see later, Rousseau had to have a model when he painted a portrait and, whoever it may have been, he could very well have pretended that he was painting *him*. Did the sitter acquire the portrait? And did Pierre Loti ever suspect its existence? All we know is that several years later the writer Georges Courteline, who was a humorist and a prankster, bought it for his private "chamber of horrors." However, before very long Rousseau's posthumous fame brought Courteline too good an offer to refuse. We all know today what amazing fluctuations of value and reputation occur in art history, but few paintings can have undergone so abrupt a reversal as this one: from a practical joker's private chamber of horrors to the walls of a museum *(see note 1, page 310)*.

Where Rousseau is concerned we must get used to the unexpected, but if we are not to lose our way constantly, we must keep tracing such facts as we possess back to their origins. The portrait of Pierre Loti expresses, above all, Rousseau's desire to attract attention to himself as a painter. The same was true of his participation in a competition organized by the municipality of Paris in October 1892, which awarded him a silver medal. At about the same time, he sent a painting to a child-health exhibition and received an honorable mention. Such trifling distinctions meant a great deal to the Douanier; fifteen years later, in a letter of 1907, he was still referring to them. In his own eyes they justified his faith in himself—and, paradoxically, for all his naïveté, he was perfectly right and his critics were all wrong. "Good old Rousseau, whose naïveté convulses the saddest people with laughter," wrote the critic for *La Nation* on the occasion of the Salon of 1892. And good old Rousseau, the innocent, cut out the passage and pasted it in his scrapbook. Do you suppose he gave it much notice? Next to it is another clipping: "M. Rousseau is one figure in the Salon des Indépendants you can't overlook," Henri Morel wrote in *Le Petit Moniteur*, "and we are happy to report that he has made real progress during the past year." Whatever the opinions, the Douanier had a peculiarity that constitutes the strength of all innocents: he could not see himself through others' eyes.

And now, this complexly simple man was about to meet and associate with the most ambiguous, the most elusive writer of the period—Alfred Jarry. It was the author of *Ubu-Roi* who actually launched the career of the ex-customs clerk as an artist, who served as link between Rousseau and the literary circles. Thanks to him the Douanier stepped out of the narrow confines of his unfashionable quarter and the isolation of the Salon des Indépendants. From this moment on, Jarry's anything but ordinary personality is superimposed over Rousseau's already incomprehensible one. Our many-faceted image of the painter now moves into the light of legend and sparkles there. Was Jarry making fun of Rousseau or did he take him seriously? The question can scarcely be answered, for to Jarry mockery was equivalent to the highest seriousness. Jarry's most ardent admirer today would tell us that this is not the way to put the question in the first place, that only the points of intersection between the grotesque and the serious are important, and that the fundamental value of Rousseau's art consists in the impossibility of defining it—as is also the case with Jarry's work. For my part, however, I feel that such an attitude, for all its elasticity, is outdated. If Jarry had expressed himself only in his conduct—being content to act out the role of Ubu, for example, in ordinary life—then, and only then, would we be obliged to respect his ambiguity, never settling any of the questions it raised. I shall formulate the problem of the relations between Rousseau and Jarry in logical terms, and I shall address myself to it using the customary means of investigation. Thus, before establishing whether Jarry did or did not ascribe any value to Rousseau, I should want to ask whether Jarry did or did not ascribe any value whatever to art, apart from the corrosive value that was properly his own, *i. e.*, Ubu-Jarry's. A lecture on "Art and Time," which he gave at the Salon des Indépendants in 1901, leaves no doubt about his position. Like everyone else, Jarry believed in art, and he believed in it with more intelligence than others—with his own more acute and probing form of intelligence.

Observing that a painting captures and records a moment of living time, its most plastic moment, Jarry contrasted painting with literature, which must

Sawmill near Paris, 1890–93

show the objects it describes one by one in succession. Then he goes on to condemn historical faithfulness in reconstructing the past, and he proves that since the work of art aims at escaping from time, it is preferable to be aware of this and to give free rein to one's imagination. In support of this he cites several examples (the elder Bruegel, the Gothic masters, prehistoric man), all of which testify to the breadth of his culture as well as to his determination to criticize the humanism of his day. In short, Jarry implicitly declares himself in favor of the incongruous in art, the creative act manifested "in the raw."

I think it is from this point of view that we should envisage Jarry's interest in the Douanier. Ubu's eccentricities do not come into the matter. Rousseau's painting was not just one of a number of grotesque objects with which Jarry surrounded himself. It marks an advanced point in his intuition. However, it has been so mixed up with the Ubuesque bric-à-brac that for many years Rousseau's biographers have been baffled. In point of fact, it was through Jarry that Rousseau re-entered the history of his times. Jarry never made fun of Rousseau, despite the fact that Jarry by this time was inseparable from his own creation, Ubu. It is the latter circumstance which is at the root of the ambiguity we feel —the more intensely for the fact that Rousseau, too, was a highly unusual artist. It is scarcely surprising that their meeting gave rise to a legend. The Douanier's fate has been the unusual one of seeming more obscure the more famous he has become—his obscurity is punctuated with contradictory questions calling for contradictory answers.

Meeting with Alfred Jarry: *War*

The two men met around 1893. Rousseau was almost fifty, a lonely man who had little beyond an elementary-school education. Jarry, a brilliant young man, was twenty years old and had come to Paris intending to enter the Ecole Normale. Already Jarry had been admitted to the circle around the *Mercure de France*, the most significant magazine of the period, which had been founded a short time before. Rousseau and Jarry had nothing whatever in common, save for the fact that they had both been born in the town of Laval. Since the actual

The Artillerymen, about 1893

BATAILLE DES PYRAMIDES.

20 *The Battle of the Pyramids*, by Georgin. Color print *(image d'Épinal)*. Inspired Rousseau's *War*

circumstances of their meeting remain unknown, the gap has been filled in by legend. First it was claimed that Rousseau and Jarry had already met in Laval, though this version was amended a little later: the painter had never known Jarry, but he had known Jarry's father. Efforts were made to suggest that the poet was behind Rousseau's decision to devote himself to painting, but comparison of their respective ages quickly ruled this out. Next, the story was circulated that Jarry had seen the Douanier standing in front of one of his paintings at the Salon des Indépendants, and that his sense of the comic had been irresistibly aroused. Finally, and perhaps most plausibly, it had been conjectured that since Rousseau and Jarry lived in the same quarter of Paris, not too far from each other, they had run into each other, discovered they were fellow townsmen, and Jarry was brought home to see Rousseau's painting. It is a fact that very early in their acquaintance Jarry commissioned him to do a lithograph *(fig. 21)* for the magazine *L'Imagier* he was preparing with Rémy de Gourmont, the first number of which appeared in September 1894. I write "very early in their acquaintance" because, although the lithograph was not published until January 1895, there is reason to believe that it was executed early in 1894, for it is clearly a preliminary sketch for the famous painting *War (colorplate, page 55)*, which was exhibited at the Salon des Indépendants in April 1894. Furthermore—and this is a point which has not been noticed until now—the subject of the lithograph, faithfully reproduced in the painting, brings

21 *War*. Lithograph by Rousseau, printed in *L'Imagier*, January 1895

to mind an *image d'Épinal* (color print) which was published in *L'Imagier*. Since this presupposes that Rousseau knew Jarry at the time, it also proves that the two men met at the beginning of 1894 at the latest. But since we are now touching on an extremely controversial subject—certain writers have gone so far as to allege that *War* is a fake Rousseau—I think we must keep to the facts as closely as possible.

Rémy de Gourmont, the theoretician of Symbolism, was one of the first to recognize Jarry's originality. Even before *Ubu-Roi* had been published (1896), Rémy de Gourmont chose the young Alfred Jarry to be his co-editor of the luxurious magazine *L'Imagier*. It was a quarterly devoted to prints, both old and new, which were often supplied with commentaries. Jarry had always been interested in art, and he was anything but a passive collaborator. His first book, *Les Minutes de Sable Mémorial*, published in 1894, and the next one, *César-Antéchrist*, published in 1895, were illustrated with his own woodcuts as well as with others that had been printed in *L'Imagier*. This is sufficient proof that Jarry's own taste was in harmony with the aesthetic tendency of the magazine. Some Jarry specialists even maintain that he, rather than Rémy de Gourmont, was the real spirit behind *L'Imagier*, notwithstanding the latter's great reputation at the time. It is not hard to go along with this view, for the magazine is a faithful image of Jarry, and after *L'Imagier* ceased publication he went on by himself to found an analogous, still more luxurious magazine which he baptized *Perhindérion*, from a Breton word meaning "pilgrimage." He squandered a good part of his inheritance on this latter magazine, bringing out the only two issues which ever appeared.

Rousseau's lithograph appeared in *L'Imagier*; in the table of contents the title is given as "War." That it was not just a commission, but a very specific commission, we shall see when we examine the magazine's policy, as expounded by Rémy de Gourmont in the leading article of the first issue: "Pictures and only pictures, religious or legendary, with just enough words to explain what they mean and to engage the minds of casual viewers." To this end, the prints were grouped by subjects—the Passion, the Virgin, Men on Horseback, and so forth—so as to evoke visual associations between different versions of the same subject. This was an incontestably modern style of presentation. The magazine was also unusual in calling attention to the most ordinary colored prints of popular origin, known in France as *images d'Épinal*. "These colored prints, which turn up on separate sheets and as pages in books, are well known to archaeologists and a few art lovers," Rémy de Gourmont writes. "They are our principal subject matter—the rest of *L'Imagier* will merely be in the way of supplement or ornamentation to them, throwing light on their origins or supplying a basis for study and comparison." Thus it came about that the magazine published Emile Bernard's engravings, whose archaism must have appealed to Rémy de Gourmont—a passionate admirer of the Middle Ages—a woodcut by Gauguin, and Rousseau's lithograph.

This lithograph was the last of a series which opened with a color print by Georgin entitled *The Battle of the Pyramids (fig. 20)*, showing Napoleon's troops drawn up in the face of the Egyptian cavalry. This was followed by several woodcuts of horsemen, after which came Rousseau's *War* (double-page spread), showing a strange-looking woman soaring on horseback over piles of corpses. The viewer who abandons himself to his visual associations is surprised when, leafing through the magazine, he discovers similarities between this lithograph and Georgin's engraving. Many details—the corpses, their position, the brandished sword, the horse's mane, the little crest between its ears (wrongly interpreted by Rousseau), its panting tongue (which recalls the prominent bits on the harnesses of the horses in *The Battle of the Pyramids)*—suggest that when Jarry asked Rousseau for a lithograph he must have shown him Georgin's color print. And since the elements of this lithograph reappear in the large painting which was exhibited in 1894—although the lithograph was not published in *L'Imagier* until 1895—we may safely assume that it was executed early in 1894 and that it served as a preliminary sketch for the painting. For my part, I am inclined to think that even the generous dimensions of the painting bespeak the fact that Rousseau was greatly encouraged by Jarry. Clearly, Rousseau breathes self-confidence; never before had he painted so large a canvas, nor would he do so again more than two or three times in his career, and then always under exceptional circumstances. Jarry's interest exalted Rousseau

War, 1894

and it was far from being as ephemeral as is supposed. Certainly it was not confined to publication of the lithograph. In its first issue (October 1894), *L'Imagier* mentioned an exhibition, "Chez le Barc de Boutteville," of the painters Filiger, Henri de Groux, Robertson, Rousseau (studies), and O'Connor, advising its readers to consult the catalogue. Unfortunately, we have been unable to find a copy of this catalogue, but since the name of Rousseau appears with those of Filiger and O'Connor, both of whom contributed to *L'Imagier*, hardly anyone but the Douanier could have been referred to here. We thus learn that in 1894 the latter exhibited "studies" in an avant-garde gallery—and there is every reason to believe that Jarry arranged this for him.

Finally, there cannot be the slightest doubt that the article on Rousseau which was published in the *Mercure de France* for March 1895 was inspired by Jarry, who we know was a close friend of Rachilde and her husband, Alfred Valette, managing editor of the *Mercure*. The article, written by L. Roy, is well worth quoting in full, although it has rarely been quoted at all. It is the only important article on Rousseau published during his lifetime and contains the following passage:

"At the exhibition of the Artistes Indépendants in 1894, Rousseau's *War* was certainly the most remarkable painting. Though it is not completely finished, not a perfect work, still, with all due deference, it represents a courageous attempt to create a symbol in the true sense of the term. The artist who painted it once again reveals his personality: all that could make it seem strange is that it recalls nothing we have ever seen before. Yet is this not a highly admirable quality? Why should strangeness provoke mockery? No one has the right to make fun of any artistic effort. Even if the effort is unsuccessful—which is not the case here—mockery is an unjust mark of pettiness. All too often in our society, people have been taught from childhood to classify, number, and label everything. Everything under the sun has to be pigeonholed, and whatever can't be baffles and perturbs people. Unable to understand, they call 'absurd' whatever escapes their categories. With a bluntness which passes for modesty with them, they maintain the proposition: 'We do not understand it, therefore it is stupid.' Despite the indisputable progress of the human race—fairly obvious today with the telegraph, the telephone, the bicycle, and the scenic railway—we are less tolerant than our forefathers in the Middle Ages, who respected the misunderstood personality with their *credo quia absurdum*.

"Rousseau has suffered the fate of all innovators. His roots are in himself alone: he possesses what is today the very rare quality of being absolutely personal. He is trying to create a new art. His attempt is on the whole very interesting, despite certain weaknesses, and in parts reveals qualities of greatness—his blacks, for instance, are very beautiful. The horizontally based composition is well conceived. The huge black horse galloping across the canvas is anything but banal. It is even a bravura performance. The figure personifying war astride the horse brandishes a sword in her right hand and holds a flaming torch in her left. On the ground lie the bodies of ordinary people, fat ones and thin ones, poor devils, proletarians. All are dead or dying. Those still breathing express the height of terror. Nature is nowhere present—except for two trees stripped of all foliage, one gray and the other black, and a few carrion crows which, attracted by the smell of blood, have swooped down to gorge themselves with the flesh of the victims of war. The ground is littered with formless debris. The earth no longer produces any vegetation, not a single blade of grass. The painting expresses well the desolation caused by irreparable disaster. Soon, not one living thing will be left, for the distant glow on the horizon tells us that fire is on its way to finish off what the sword began. Shortly, the desolation will have become total, final. War gallops on over the scene, impassive, inexorable, like some implacable divinity—on and on, no carnage great enough to appease her. Nothing can stop her frenzied course. What an obsession, what a nightmare! What a painful impression of insurmountable sadness! Only bad faith could lead one to believe that the man capable of suggesting such ideas to us is a bad artist."

As with the other articles about him, Rousseau pasted this one in his scrapbook. We can scarcely imagine what it must have meant to him. Jarry's appearance on the scene had helped him enormously. When, just about this time, he painted the *Portrait of Jarry*, which was exhibited at the Salon des Indépendants in April 1895, he must have worked with exceptional care and fervor. Unfortunately, the portrait has not come down to us. As legend has it, Jarry, "no longer distinguishing Ubu from himself," used it as a target in revolver practice, and destroyed the canvas "for the purely literary pleasure of slashing his own likeness, rolling it up, and putting it away in a drawer to show to distinguished visitors." Apollinaire partly confirms the story, writing that the portrait was partially burned and that in 1906 when he saw it, only "the very expressive head" remained. He also tells us that Jarry was depicted with "a parrot, and the famous chameleon which for a time was his companion." No matter how carefully we pore over the newspaper descriptions at the time of its exhibition, we learn little more than this, apart from a few indications as to colors used, and so forth. "It is a portrait with the figure next to a window through which daylight streams. The man is of a light zinc color, seated at a little table of the same color, with a dirty face, against a background of yellow drapery on which are painted human figures and animals of all kinds." Such was the description in *Le Gaulois*. It is supplemented by one in *Le Temps*: "On the balcony near which the poet is shown seated, we find an owl and a screech-owl. A number of emblems around him disclose that his are not the concerns of the vulgar herd. A pen stuck behind his ear shows that he is a writer by profession. His round, fixed, black eyes, his implacably black hair, and his formal attire, also black, further emphasize the seriousness of his habitual preoccupations." The "pen" mentioned in *Le Temps* was apparently a mistake, for in *L'Idée moderne*, a magazine for the young, we find: "The poet, dressed in black, is shown seated. Around him are his favorite animals—owls and a chameleon. The chameleon's tongue was mistaken by one art critic for a pen."

All we know about the famous portrait of Jarry is contained in these few lines. One further bit of information must have delighted Jarry at the time. Because of his long hair, the portrait was listed in the catalogue as *Portrait of Madame A. J.* Lastly, we know that the following quatrain was inscribed on the gilt frame:

> *Muses dont le front de rêve est un triangle lapidaire,*
> *Ornez ses yeux de votre image, afin qu'il puisse toujours plaire*
> *Aux lecteurs, cherchant dans un esprit sincère*
> *A goûter agréablement ce qui donne la lumière.*

> [Muses whose dreamy forehead is a lapidary triangle,
>   Adorn his eyes with your image, that he may always please
>   Readers who try, in a sincere spirit,
>   Pleasantly to savor that which light can give.]

"Though lacking harmony and rhythm, the quatrain has an indefinable, inspired quality, which touches the heart and clearly comes from a noble soul," wrote the critic in *Le Temps*. He went on to ask: "But who wrote the quatrain? The painter or the poet? The reader, as we do, must regret not knowing."

As for Rousseau, he was once again derided. "Go see the Rousseaus, O my readers—lots of fun for your one-franc admission!" wrote the art critic on the *National*. He was echoed in *Le Gaulois:* "M. Rousseau certainly could not have painted it with his hands." Only Lormel, the critic on *L'Idée moderne* (he must have admired Jarry), spoke of Rousseau in a different tone: "M. Rousseau ... too, is an innovator, since *L'Imagier* publishes his works. In any case, M. Rousseau is a sincere, dedicated man. He is primitive because he cannot paint otherwise."

The two epithets, "sincere" and "dedicated," are particularly appropriate to the painter's psychological development during these years. Nothing reflects his state of mind as faithfully and movingly as the autobiography he wrote, hoping for publication. In 1894, the first volume of *Portraits du prochain siècle*, containing short biographies of contemporary writers, had appeared. A second volume, devoted to painters and sculptors, was in preparation. The Douanier called personally on the publisher, Girard-Coutances, and submitted the following text:

HENRI ROUSSEAU
Painter

Born in Laval in 1844, he was obliged at first, in view of his parents' lack of means, to follow a career different from that to which his artistic tastes called him.

Child on the Rocks, after 1895

Therefore it was not until 1885 that he made his debut in Art after many disappointments, alone and without any master but nature and some advice from Gérôme and Clément. His first two creations exhibited were sent to the Salon des Champs-Elysées and were entitled *Italian Dance* and *Sunset*.

The following year he painted *Carnival Evening* and *Thunderclap*. And then, *Waiting*, *A Poor Devil*, *After the Banquet*, *Departure*, *Dinner on the Grass*, *Suicide*, *To My Father*, *Myself: Portrait-Landscape of the Author*, *Scouts Attacked by a Tiger*, *The Centenary of Independence*, *Freedom*, *The Last Man of the 51st*, *War*, a Genre Portrait of the Writer *A. J.*, about two hundred pen-and-pencil drawings, and a number of landscapes of Paris and environs.

It is only after very great hardships that he succeeded in making himself known to the numerous artists now around him. He has improved himself more and more in the original style which he has adopted and he is in the process of becoming one of our best realist painters.

As a characteristic feature, he wears a bushy beard and has long been a member of the Indépendants, convinced that any pioneer whose thoughts aspire to the beautiful and the good should be permitted to create in complete freedom.

He will never forget the members of the press who have been able to understand him and have supported him in his moments of discouragement, and who will have helped to make him what he must become.

Written in Paris, July 10, 1895.

Attached was an ink drawing of himself *(fig. 6)* to serve as an illustration when the autobiography was printed. However, the projected volume never came out—a typical event in the Douanier's life, it being his fate always to be outside of his times. When, miraculously, a document like this one accidentally escapes destruction, it is like a breath of fresh air. At last we have the Douanier himself, without intermediaries, just as he really was, and we need not attempt to deduce attitudes by elaborate reconstruction and inference. Here is the man with "the bushy beard" and a "member of the Indépendants," as he casually lets fall, the one we could not otherwise track down. The Douanier knows that his career has advanced. He looks back at the past, mentions "great hardships," and since there is no place for modesty in naïveté, he calmly asserts that he is "in process of becoming one of our best realist painters" without the slightest embarrassment. His phrasing in the third person implicates the presumed writer and makes the latter subscribe to the flattering opinion. It is a truth so self-evident to Rousseau that he states it without the slightest fuss: he is great, and so he is devoted to the freedom of art—"any pioneer whose thoughts aspire to the beautiful and the good should be permitted to create in complete freedom." But his good heart contains still other ideas—"He will never forget the members of the press . . . who will have helped to make him what he must become."

The Quarry, about 1896–97

We cannot help thinking of Don Quixote tilting at windmills when we look at the date—July 10, 1895! And this is Rousseau himself speaking! He will never cease to surprise us, but there is something extraordinary about this surprise: in 1895 Don Quixote speaks of himself precisely as he will be spoken of fifty years later. When we look at his self-confidence against the scanty background of facts which could have encouraged it, we are simply stunned. All we can say is what his friend Jarry said of him: *le mirifique Rousseau* (Rousseau the miracle worker).

The Douanier was becoming more assured in his daily habits as well. He personally called on the publisher with his autobiographical sketch, and although it must have been Jarry who tipped him off about the forthcoming volume, still Rousseau sat down and wrote his own portrait in words. More and more his life reflected his status as a recognized artist. In his scrapbook he noted: "April 12, visit to M. Serendat de Belzim's exhibition at the Georges Petit gallery," and he adds, "very good." What could he possibly have seen in the work of this utterly forgotten artist? The gallery was a fashionable one, the artist was greatly in demand in the salons, and he was a fellow member of the Indépendants—indeed, treasurer of the group. The event was one to be remembered—like the annual banquet held by the members of the Indépendants. It was written up in the newspapers: "At the dessert ... M. Rousseau, the most independent painter of the organization, who exhibits at the Palais des Arts Libéraux canvases such as have never been seen elsewhere, sang an aria from *Mignon*."

This is the earliest reference to Rousseau's other talent. Besides being a painter and author of a comedy, he was also a musician. He had won a prize for his singing at the Lycée. It would seem, however, that his musical knowledge was not confined to the rudiments learned at school. Whether as a result of the creative upsurge he experienced from 1895 on, or inspiration gained from the transcriptions of old folk songs, motets, and roundelays which were being published in *L'Imagier*, the fact remains that the Douanier took up music and composed the waltz *Clémence*, which has come down to us. His was an over-flowing temperament likely to seek out additional means of expression—we have already seen this in connection with his play about the 1889 World's Fair. *Clémence* is a sentimental waltz for violin or mandolin, which was published in 1904. However, it could not have been composed later than 1899, when he married for the second time, because it bears the name of his first wife. It seems likely to me that it was the product of high spirits during 1895 and 1896, the leisure-time occupation of a happy man, confident of his powers as a painter.

In his scrapbook we find inscribed, like a landmark, the single entry "April 10, 1894," and a calling card pasted above it: "Alfred Jarry, 78 Bd du Port Royal." Nothing else. Then come new clippings, and the page is filled. The Douanier's career continues apace.

The pictures he submitted to the Indépendants in 1896 seem to have driven the critics to new heights (or depths) of abuse. A painting which has been lost, bearing the title *A Philosopher*, was their main target. "Here is a man who scorns all schools," we read in *L'Éclair*, "all conventions, even the most elementary ones, such as form, color, composition, perspective, etc." And for the reader's amusement, the critic quoted in their entirety some verses by the Douanier which accompanied the picture:

> *Quoique ne vivant pas dans un tonneau*
> *Je suis comme le Juif-Errant sur la terre*
> *Ne craignant ni la bourrasque ni l'eau*
> *Trottinant, tout en fumant ma vieille pipe,*
> *Bravant avec fierté la foudre, le tonnerre,*
> *Pour gagner une somme modique*
> *Malgré que la pluie mouille par terre*
> *Je porte sur mon dos et sans réplique*
> *L'annonce du journal indépendant.*

> [Although I do not live in a barrel
> I am like the Wandering Jew
> Fearing neither wind nor water,
> Trotting about smoking my old pipe,
> Proudly braving the thunder and lightning,
> Just to earn a modest sum.
> Despite the rain that is drenching the ground
> I carry on my back, unanswerably,
> The advertisement for the independent newspaper.]

The poem clearly shows that the "philosopher" was a sandwich man. This form of advertising must have struck the Douanier's imagination, and his reaction is very interesting: to him the philosopher, the superior man, is the one who rises above his humiliating condition. (This reaction must be kept in mind, for it may contain an autobiographical element, as we shall see later.)

As for other reviewers, they outdid themselves in irony. Rousseau was "a victim of the brush," he "paints so as to make his contemporaries shake with laughter," his "portraits and landscapes are made to cheer up hypochondriacs and persons whose lives are careworn."

Imperturbable, the Douanier kept right on working. Shortly, he was to paint one of the most interesting works of the century, *The Sleeping Gypsy* (*colorplate, page 65*), which he exhibited in 1897.

22   *The Two Majesties*, by Léon Gérôme

The Sleeping Gypsy, 1897

The Sleeping Gypsy

This painting stands out so remarkably from the rest of Rousseau's work that it has baffled posterity as well as his contemporaries, though perplexed admiration has gradually supplanted gibes and jeers. Like *War*, it disappeared from sight for many years, and when it turned up again in 1923 in the Quinn collection, it provoked endless discussion and comments ranging from "a masterpiece" to "a fake." Twelve years later, in 1935, when Rousseau's letter describing the picture and giving its dimensions was published, new doubts arose: the dimensions given by Rousseau were not those of the painting. It was concluded that the work we know was not the one exhibited in 1897, but a second version of the same subject. Closer investigation, however, showed that the canvas had at some time been mounted on a smaller stretcher, its edges folded back, the folds corresponding to the dimensions given by Rousseau. But opinion is still divided; it is a work that repels rational considerations, that appears to be irreducible to other terms.

However, it is not altogether unrelated to the Douanier's life, although references to the artist's everyday world are far from obvious. The fact is, that in this work the ordinary, day-by-day sources of inspiration have been transfigured in the highest degree through the power of painting. As we have seen, Rousseau was deeply impressed by the World's Fair. Jarry did not change Rousseau's tastes or habits—he merely gave him self-confidence, made him freer, much freer. When Rousseau let his imagination go, the result was *The Sleeping Gypsy*. This strange painting goes back, on the one hand, to *The Two Majesties (fig. 22)* by Gérôme, Rousseau's "teacher" (note that in his autobiographical sketch he mentioned Gérôme before Clément: in 1895 Gérôme came first in his eyes). On the other hand, it recalls stories about gypsies which were very much in vogue at the time. There may have been something about a traveling carnival of gypsies that had a lion (such animals could be picked up from menageries cutting down on their stock or being sold due to bankruptcy). Every cliché about gypsies is to be found in the painting. They are nomads—witness the jar and the stick; they are strangely dressed—notice the strange striped garment; they often play instruments to earn a living—see the mandolin; they are sometimes credited with magical powers—witness the lion who sniffs at the gypsy yet does not devour her. It is a perfect example of art refining and improving on anecdote.

At the Salon des Indépendants of 1897, *The Sleeping Gypsy* was the main attraction. The critics rose to the occasion as usual: "M. Rousseau's *Sleeping Gypsy* is a pure masterpiece! At the bottom of it we read, 'The feline, though ferocious, hesitates to jump at its prey who, out of exhaustion, has fallen asleep.'" Visitors to the exhibition laughed themselves sick. Other reviews took this tack: "M. Rousseau has decided to settle for the easy fame of making an utter fool of himself."

As for Rousseau, he behaved as if he were completely deaf. Indeed, it was this painting, the object of so many jeers, which he offered to sell to his native town! Was he so convinced he had created a masterpiece? Just what importance did he ascribe to it, such as led him to write to the mayor of Laval asking him to buy it? It seems to me that several issues may be involved, and it would be helpful to look into them one by one.

When the Salon closed, Rousseau took his pictures home. There, in front of the wall full of paintings, a long confrontation must have taken place between *The Sleeping Gypsy* and Jarry. In a letter to one of his creditors, dated August 23, 1897, Jarry says that he is staying temporarily "in the house of a friend, M. Rousseau." (He had purchased a bicycle, did not meet his payments, had been served a summons, and had moved out of his own apartment.) Rousseau's kindheartedness and generosity are well known: on this point all testimonies agree. We learn from another letter that on September 15, still penniless, Jarry was still staying with Rousseau. Thus, for at least three weeks he lived with *The Sleeping Gypsy* in front of him. And it is certain that his reactions to the painting were not those it had provoked at the Salon. His thirst for the unusual could not have been disappointed. Who can tell whether it was not at this time that the idea of selling the painting to the municipality of Laval was born? Surely, two topics must have been discussed often by these two natives of that town—painting and money. However, Rousseau did not write to the mayor until a year later and in the meantime he had exhibited five new paintings at the Indépendants. Still, he did not offer any of them—he offered *The Sleeping Gypsy*. The letter the Douanier wrote on this occasion has the same touching mixture of naïveté and self-assurance that characterizes all his writings:

July 10, 1898

Monsieur le Maire,

I have the honor of sending you these few lines as a native of your town, who has become a self-taught artist and is desirous that his native city possess one of his works, proposing that you purchase from me a genre painting entitled *The Sleeping Gypsy*, which measures 2 m. 60 in width and 1m. 90 in height. A wandering Negress, who plays the mandolin, with her jar next to her (a vase containing drinking water), is deeply asleep, worn out from fatigue. A lion happens to go by, sniffs at her, and does not devour her. There is an effect of moonlight, very poetic. The scene takes place in a completely arid desert. The gypsy is dressed in oriental fashion.

I will let it go for 2,000 or 1,800 francs, for I would be happy to let the town of Laval possess a remembrance of one of its children.

In the hope that my offer will be treated with favor, accept, Monsieur le Maire, the assurance of my distinguished consideration.

Henri Rousseau
Painter
3 rue Vercingétorix
Paris

Nothing came of the offer. I believe that he was moved to send it by an urgent need for money, and cannot help seeing a connection between it and his forthcoming marriage to Joséphine Noury, the widow Tensorer. They were married on September 2, 1899. In any event, the letter opens a period in his life about which we know very little. Emotional shock? Sentimental worries? Financial preoccupations? Clearly, there was some sort of crisis. For two successive years, 1899 and 1900, Rousseau did not exhibit with the Indépendants. On the other hand, he was writing. On January 5, 1899 he completed a play, *A Russian Orphan's Revenge*, and in November 1900 he took part in a painting competition at the town hall of Asnières. What happened in the interval? Had he gone on painting? We know to what extent his life was focused on painting, and we know of nothing which might have discouraged him from going on, so it seems as though he must have been entirely caught up in something else. Possibly it was his love for the woman he finally married. The play he wrote would point in this direction—we have already seen how his overflowing enthusiasm for the World's Fair had moved him to write. *A Russian Orphan's Revenge* reveals him trying very hard to be a writer, but in transposing his preoccupations, he betrays himself—his clumsiness as a writer gives him away. We find the stubborn self-taught worker, the man who lacks all sense of time, and who continually flies in the face of the impossible. Much in the play simply takes for granted conditions contrary to possibility; the action and the characters have the quality of a marionette show. Rousseau's patriotism pours out in a long tirade; his comic verve reveals itself the moment he brings common people onto the stage. At the other extreme the tone is false, affected with all sorts of artificial graces of language, when he presents his principal characters who belong to the upper classes. Rousseau was unfamiliar with the latter; that he chose to write about them at all bespeaks his ambitions; he writes as seriously as he paints. And the subject he treats is a drama of love and money.

The sentimental reasons which might have inspired the play are more or less detectable. Not so clear are his motives for adding the name of Mme Barkovsky as coauthor, after he had completed the play. Possibly this lady with the Slavic name supplied Rousseau with useful information about Russia, where the action takes place. In this case, however, the Douanier was being much too kind when he listed her as coauthor. We can hardly keep from wondering whether Joséphine herself might supply the key to this riddle, if only her identity could be investigated more closely. She might give us as well an answer to

Banks of the Seine, about 1898

another riddle, for a Yadwigha appears among the characters in the play, and several years later one of Rousseau's most famous paintings was to involve a Yadwigha. On this hypothesis, not only Rousseau but also his wife may have pinned all their hopes on the success of *A Russian Orphan's Revenge*. The manuscript was in fact sent to the Châtelet Theater, but the play was never staged. This would explain why Rousseau stopped exhibiting—especially if his wife was convinced that his talents lay rather in writing than in painting. As it is, we shall never know what was really going on during these years. Rémy de Gourmont relates that he often ran into Rousseau at various street corners on the Left Bank, playing his own tunes on the violin, and this recollection, as well as others, may date from this period: Rousseau playing in the orchestra of the Amicale of the Fifth Arrondissement, Rousseau as sales inspector for the *Petit Parisien* in his quarter, a job that involved long walks from newsstand to newsstand. He could only have done these things to add to his meager resources. According to other statements, which may well be inaccurate, for they were collected much later, his wife opened a little stationery shop where, among other things, she tried to sell Rousseau's paintings. It was at this time, when money troubles seem to have kept him from painting, that the World's Fair of 1900 was held. If it revived Rousseau's former exaltation, it could only have done so to the extent that it reawakened memories of the 1889 Fair. For times had changed. Emphasis on local color had yielded to a scientific style of presentation. In the colonial pavilions the most prominent place was given to statistics and engineering projects. Industrial exhibits supplanted the picturesque. The only traces of the past, according to the guidebook to the 1900 Fair, were "a few thickly wooded spots around the Trocadéro, dating from 1889, shady spots of unobtrusive poetic appeal." The entertainments, too, were very different. The cinema had not yet been quite perfected, but there were dioramas of all kinds, and a "mareorama" tried to reconstruct life in motion. A "cineorama" offered a bird's-eye view of Europe: visitors sat in the basket of a balloon surrounded by balloonists' gear, and when the signal for departure was given, they had the impression of taking off. The ground seemed to give way under them.

In fact, everything seemed to be giving way, as if things had lost their consistency. The world of Rousseau's youth was no more. To an ever greater extent he would summon up in his paintings the exotic settings which the 1889 Fair had revealed to him. With the voluptuousness of a man plunging into his past, which comes so close to dream, he began to paint those canvases filled with tropical vegetation and populated with wild beasts, which he exhibited from 1904 on.

In 1904 Rousseau was once again alone with his painting. His second wife died in 1903. But his solitude now was different from that which he had experienced after the death of his first wife. In 1901 he began to exhibit regularly again with the Indépendants, pasting the same kind of press cuttings as before into his scrapbook, though less methodically and with less love. His scrapbook was no longer his only link with the outside world. From 1901 on, he had been teaching drawing at the Ecole Philotechnique, located in his quarter. This was a typical establishment of the period which, in the name of progress, attempted to bring culture to the masses, though without the seriousness of adult education courses of today. Judging by the importance Rousseau attached to his classes, it would seem that he had finally found again, or thought he had found, a responsible position in society, such as he had lacked ever since he had become an artist. Possibly the new job was in part taken on to please his wife, the enigmatic Joséphine, who may well have had petty-bourgeois ambitions. It may also have been during this period that Rousseau became a Freemason—that he was one we know from a letter of 1907. The fact in itself has no special significance other than giving Rousseau further ties with the society around him. As democracy spread in France, Freemasonry trickled down to the lower classes in an increasingly politicalized form. We see that Rousseau was not nearly as pathetically alone as he had been during the years when he began to paint. Shortly after his second wife's death, he moved to the studio in the Rue Perrel, which became the setting for the best-known portions of the Rousseau legend.

The Last Years

So far, in following Rousseau's life, we have refused to be influenced by tales that purport to account for Rousseau's entire life in highly colorful detail. We have done best to grasp their limitations. Although they must in the end be branded legend, they probably are accurate when they relate otherwise unsubstantiated small fragments of fact. Thus we have learned that "sketches from nature hung among his paintings all over the Douanier's studio. They brightened up an otherwise shabby room, and to someone who asked him whether he did not mind having to live and work in one room, he replied, 'Don't you see, when I wake up, I can smile at my pictures.'" We are also told that at a certain moment there appeared on the walls several reproductions of Watteaus, others by a forgotten painter by the name of Bolouris, and the cast of an Egyptian bas-relief—but here, perhaps, memory may be less reliable. Rousseau's violin was placed conspicuously, there were a few chairs, a hideous statue, and the famous red sofa which appears in *The Dream*. The little stove on which the Douanier prepared his own meals stood there summer and winter. Witnesses also tell us that with his friend Queval (his landlord) "he would cook up a stew meant to last a whole week. But the poor people in the quarter knew when he was cooking the stew and would always drop in that day. Naturally he shared his meal with them, and then had to live the rest of the week on bread." The conclusion has often been drawn that "the Douanier's charity made him a real St. Vincent de Paul."

The Douanier has often been spoken of in this tone at once touched and touching. Something in his make-up must have provoked it, doubtless his great kindliness. Rousseau was aware of it, for in a letter of 1907 he writes: "... I helped poor people who were ashamed of being poor, gave them shelter, fed them, and on one occasion I had seven of them at my table. I found jobs for two or three invalids. As a result I was known as a good man, and people were continually appealing to me. But in the end I realized that if I went on like that, I should myself be in want. I asked the municipal councillor what to do, and he authorized me to send persons I knew to be really in need of assistance to the mayor of the 18th arrondissement.

"I did so, continuing to help as best I could the men, women, and children who kept knocking at my door. This was how I came to be called 'Père Rousseau' in the neighborhood, and I am proud of it."

As can be seen, the Douanier's kindheartedness was by no means a fiction. Everything his contemporaries tell us about him confirms this. "Rousseau was very kind and hospitable," writes Robert Delaunay. "He was happy to receive you, even when he had his palette in his hand. He would ask you to sit down, and keep on working in his white smock ....I shall never forget the leisurely hours I spent in this way as he beamingly went on working at his canvases. I was attracted by his calm, his deep satisfaction in his work. I would often go watch him work in the late afternoon."

Thanks to Robert Delaunay, his most faithful friend from the beginning, we have a description of Rousseau, the indefatigable worker: "His day started early, when he put on his smock, and he did not take it off until sunset, laying down his brush only to make himself a bite to eat." In 1905 his long working days turned out a painting that shows Rousseau in his finest form—the famous *Hungry Lion (colorplate, page 75)*. Its subject is explained point by point in the accompanying note: "The hungry lion throws himself on the antelope and devours it; the panther waits anxiously for the moment when it too will have its share. Carnivorous birds have pecked out a piece of flesh from the back of the animal, which weeps. Sunset." We feel that Rousseau gave himself completely to this vast composition. We can almost see him, filling in diligently the six square yards of canvas. But a question that inevitably arises remains unanswered: we do not know what event or person induced the Douanier to paint this picture. For, like all self-taught artists, he was timid when left wholly on his own. We

Baby's Party, 1903

have seen this repeatedly: he has self-confidence, but he is wary and his talent soars only when encouraged. He could hardly have been encouraged by the reception given the exotic landscape he exhibited the year before, in 1904, yet now he returns to the genre and triples the dimensions. "People are incapable of keeping serious in front of *Scouts Attacked by a Tiger (fig. 95)*," a reviewer commented. This rather special canvas must have aroused the enthusiasm of a prominent person, and provided the impetus Rousseau needed to produce *Hungry Lion*. It is possible that from the outset the painting had been destined for the Salon d'Automne, where it was not only accepted, but prominently hung, and noticed by the critics. We do not know whether all this came about through good luck or as the result of expert advice. In any case, this was a turning point in the Douanier's career. For three years in a row, pictures by him were included in the Salon d'Automne—mostly of exotic subjects. During the same years he continued to show more traditional works at the Salon des Indépendants. The 1905 Salon d'Automne was the turning point.

As is well known, this was the year the Fauves made their first big splash. The movement had been started in 1903 by a group of young artists who constituted the extreme avant garde. At the Salon d'Automne in 1905, Rousseau's *Hungry Lion* was hung in the central exhibition room next to paintings by Matisse, Derain, Braque, Rouault, Vlaminck, Friesz, and Dufy—and this was the room the critics baptized *la cage aux fauves* (the wild-beasts' cage). Today it is impossible to say to what extent Rousseau's picture of a wild beast (and it was a big picture) entered into the fateful naming of the movement, otherwise most remarkable for its utterly uninhibited use of color. Louis Vauxcelles, who coined the word, was rather impressed by the Douanier's work. "M. Rousseau has the rigid mentality of the Byzantine mosaicists," he wrote in *Gil Blas*, "or the tapestry makers of Bayeux. It is a pity that his technique should not be up to the level of his directness. His fresco leaves one anything but indifferent." And he was not alone in speaking of Rousseau in this tone. "It is an enlarged Persian miniature, transformed into an enormous decoration which is not devoid of merit," said *Le Temps. L'Illustration française*, on the double page it devoted to the Salon d'Automne, reproduced *Hungry Lion* together with a number of works by Cézanne, Matisse, Vuillard, Rouault, and Derain. Thus Rousseau was suddenly incorporated into the most vital artistic movement of his time. He certainly had an opportunity to meet his fellow exhibitors, but he could not develop especially close relations with any of them. To begin with, most of them were much younger than he, and, more important, Rousseau thought that their experiments were utterly wrong. He said of Matisse's work: "If it were only amusing! But it is sad, and horribly ugly!" As has often been noted, his ideal was academic painting, the kind taught at the Ecole des Beaux-Arts, and in his eyes the only desirable prizes and awards were those given by the Salon des Artistes Français—to which Bouguereau belonged. There is a story that on one occasion, when buying paint, Rousseau asked for "Bouguereau

Hungry Lion, 1905

flesh color," and that the "master's" death genuinely saddened him. Anyone who admired Bouguereau that much in 1905 could hardly make friends with the Fauves or with Cézanne. That is the way Rousseau was: a strange prism that distorted values in a way utterly his own. He is always turning up just where we least expect him.

Thus, after the Salon d'Automne closed in 1905 (where, historically speaking, his painting rightly belonged), he seems to have felt the need to assert his solidarity with the Artistes Indépendants. He now painted a work representing, as the title indicates, *Liberty Inviting the Artists to Exhibit at the 22nd Salon des Indépendants (colorplate, page 89)*, and he exhibited it in 1906, at the 22nd Salon held by that group. When we look at this painting, which must have been intended as an apotheosis of the Salon, and which is touching in its naïveté, we cannot help smiling. Once again we are face to face with the absurd. Before us is the puerile effort of a man of sixty in an earnest quest for fame, but whose fame was to come from precisely that quarter where he least expected it.

Rousseau had now been painting for twenty years, but his life was still anything but an easy one. He gave lessons in the dance, painting, and music. His calling card bore the inscription, "Classes at home, moderate prices." On another calling card we read, "Classes in drawing, painting, and watercolor— Private lessons." And he adds, "As the teacher wants to encourage progress, enrollment will be strictly limited in every class." A schedule was as follows: "Mixed classes for children and young people, Saturdays from 2 to 5.—For adults over 16, Academy, living models, Thursday evenings from 8 to 10." And as though to forestall all possible objections from people in his quarter he adds: "Parents may observe both day and evening classes. Tuition: 8 francs per month."

According to Apollinaire, the fee was later increased to 12 francs. Legend in this connection contributes the memory of two pupils—"two old men, one 72 and the other 80, who after the class was over often took him to task for having embraced such a thankless profession and advised him to go back to being an honest civil servant." Robert Delaunay more than once observed one of these old men in a corner of the studio, painting on pieces of canvas Rousseau gave him, and whose name—a crowning irony—was René Rousseau. Clearly, there was no lack of imaginative people in Rousseau's neighborhood, the Plaisance quarter, where "even the paving stones seemed to be laid down the wrong way," writes Roch Grey—a neighborhood very much in the image of Rousseau's painting, "where, on Sundays, happiness was so general and so intense that it became palpable, like the weather." But to the "respectable" people of Plaisance, the shopkeepers and men with a trade, could art ever represent anything but a pastime, a hobby? Did Rousseau earn much from his classes? All we know is that he did the best he could, until the day his paintings began to sell. The catalogue of the Salon des Indépendants for 1907 is eloquent on this score: five out of six of Rousseau's pictures are listed as belonging to private collectors; as for the sixth, it was an "official" subject which Rousseau painted with the

Salon in mind. This was the painting entitled *Representatives of the Foreign Powers Come To Salute the Republic as a Peaceful Gesture*. Iconographically, the work is reminiscent of certain photographs published in 1905 when the King of England visited Paris. With respect to the picture's content, it may have been inspired by Gérôme's painting, *Napoleon III Receiving the Siamese Ambassadors*.

Thus, in 1907, after twenty-two years of work, Rousseau suddenly sold several paintings all at one time. The same year he also received his first commission, *The Snake Charmer (colorplate, page 97)*, which he painted for the mother of his young friend and fervent admirer, Robert Delaunay. Rousseau frequented Mme Delaunay's bourgeois salon, and one day she told him about her journey to India. This inspired the painting, though it may also be based on memories of snake charmers who had shortly before attracted attention at the Cirque Molier. The work was exhibited at the Salon des Indépendants and was well received. The Douanier must have been happy—success was coming at last.

Then, misfortune struck. On December 2, 1907, Henri Rousseau was arrested "for forgery and embezzlement." "He did not seem to realize the seriousness of his situation," says Maurice Garçon, the lawyer to whom we owe a detailed study of Rousseau's trial. "The fact is, he could perfectly well have been sentenced to a term of hard labor."

The Trial

In October 1907, a man named Sauvaget came to see Rousseau. The latter had known him as a member of the Amicale of the Fifth Arrondissement, but he had not seen him for years. Sauvaget told him that the bankers had stripped him of all his possessions and that in order to recover them he needed Rousseau's help. Considering the kind of adversary he had to deal with, the method he planned to use was a banking transaction. Rousseau agreed to help. Sauvaget, about thirty, was a clerk at a branch of the Bank of France in Meaux, and what he was actually planning was the theft of a considerable sum of money. He needed an accomplice, however, and he picked Rousseau for this role.

It would have been a clever fraud. All Rousseau had to do was to follow Sauvaget's instructions. He went to Lyon, and there made a small deposit in the local branch of the Bank of France, opening an account under a false name. However, when the bank refused to give him a checkbook, he withdrew his deposit. Sauvaget next sent him to Laon to repeat the same operation, but once again the deposit was insufficient to entitle him to a checkbook. Sauvaget then had him write to the Laon branch requesting that the deposit be mailed to him in Paris, care of General Delivery. To collect the sum at the post office, however, Rousseau had to show his marriage certificate in order to identify himself. The same operation was attempted a third time at Melun, and this time was successful: Rousseau received a checkbook in the name of Bailly. Then Sauvaget instructed him to order special blanks and envelopes with the letterheads of the Bank of France, and he used the stationery to notify the Meaux branch that a depositor of the Melun branch by name of Bailly would present a check for 21,000 francs, and that the check could be honored, since the deposit in Melun was sufficient to cover it. Rousseau, equipped with false documents given him by Sauvaget, went to Meaux and withdrew the money. He kept 1,000 francs and handed the remaining 20,000 to Sauvaget. The fraud had been successfully perpetrated. But what was Rousseau's part in all this? Was he really a dupe? Did he really believe he was just doing a favor for a friend, thereby earning a sizable amount of money? Once again we are faced with Rousseau's characteristic style: he was not an accomplice, exactly, nor was he exactly altogether taken in. As a "criminal" he was just as unmistakably himself as in everything else, as his behavior in prison and at the trial attests.

The Bank of France discovered the fraud very quickly, and the police easily traced the nonexistent Bailly to the Henri Rousseau who had identified himself at the General Delivery window of the post office. This was really the only flaw in an otherwise well-managed swindle. Rousseau was arrested in December 1907.

What did he do once he found himself in a cell at the Santé prison? He sat down and wrote several long letters, six addressed to the investigating magistrate and one to his municipal councillor. These letters are our richest source of information about his personality, his past, and his character—veritable cornerstones of the Rousseau biography. That we have even so much as this in the way of documents, we owe to officialdom's passion for keeping files on everything related to courtroom cases. Tracked down and published by Maître Garçon in 1953, these letters provide us with our most substantial evidence, and we have already drawn on them in these pages.

Rousseau at once made a clean breast of everything, and Sauvaget, who also confessed at once, exonerated him of all responsibility. So Rousseau set about writing to the investigating magistrate, pleading for leniency. Appealing to the judge's compassion, he spoke about the kind of life he had led and described himself as a great painter "known favorably in all the Paris galleries." The most interesting fact about these letters is their insistence. Rousseau wrote the first letter December 5, and the very next morning, Friday, December 6, he wrote the second. He was in a hurry to be released; he was expected to show up

The Lane, about 1905

Sunday morning for his class at the Ecole Philotechnique. "You will be kind enough not to destroy a career so laboriously acquired," he wrote in his first letter; and in the second: "I have my class to teach day after tomorrow, a class in drawing, watercolor, and painting which cannot be held at night. My pupils are counting on me and will be there waiting for me." Then, as though upon reflection he realized some sort of compromise might be necessary, he added a postscript :"If you refuse to release me for my class, then please have me escorted." And he goes on to say, "Why did this young man have to come along and disturb my life—the last thing I needed?" The letter closes with this pathetic question.

We easily recognize the Douanier's style, his way of jumping from one subject to the other without transition, of advancing completely irrelevant arguments—as when he notes that his class could not be held at night. Did he suppose that it would be easier to obtain the judge's permission to attend if the class *were* held at night, or that he would be released from prison on a Sunday night? The same "style" was in evidence at the trial. Rousseau was released provisionally on December 31, 1907; the case came up for trial only a year later, on January 9, 1909. Seated in the dock with Sauvaget, he did not look intimidated. His counsel, Maître Guilhermet, produced one of his paintings—an exotic landscape. The courtroom laughed. Rousseau's scrapbook was introduced, and the anonymous quatrain in tribute to the painter was read aloud. The audience laughed again. Then the painter Maximilien Luce testified in favor of Rousseau, praising his work. After Maître Guilhermet, the defense counsel, made his plea, Rousseau was plainly heard to say to him, "Look, now that you're through, can't I go?" The courtroom shook with laughter. The judge read the verdict. Rousseau was given a suspended sentence of two years and fined 100 francs. The aged painter was satisfied. "Thank you, your Honor," he said, "I'll do the portrait of your lady." George Clarétie wrote in *Le Figaro*: "And there was not the least bit of irony in his sincere and moving expression of gratitude." Rousseau had had a narrow escape: the preliminary investigation had failed to unearth the conviction for larceny recorded when he was nineteen, and he himself may have forgotten it. It was a part of his past that had been swallowed up by painting.

Thanks to his trial, we have a description of Rousseau: "Age 63, but looks between 50 and 54. Medium height: about 1 m 65 cm, average corpulence, dark brown hair streaked with gray, fairly thick not very long mustache, dark brown, also very gray, average build, pale complexion with a few reddish spots, eyes rather deep-set, walks head forward, has the air of an ailing man; at present wears his hair short, formerly wore it long."

The man so described in the police report is the man whom Apollinaire, Roch Grey, Salmon, and Picasso knew at just about this time.

Rousseau and Apollinaire

No document enables us to establish when Rousseau met Apollinaire. It is probable that they were introduced to each other by Jarry who, in a letter addressed to Apollinaire in April 1906 (published in *Soirées de Paris*, May 15, 1914), wrote: "See you soon, I hope, and then we'll make the mirific expedition to Rousseau's. I was supposed to lunch with him Wednesday but I was so busy I couldn't make it." Consequently, the meeting between Apollinaire and Rousseau must have taken place between April 1906 and November 1907, the date of Jarry's death. In any event, by 1908 they were seeing each other regularly. It seems that the Douanier even kept a special notebook for his appointments with this illustrious friend, the young poet who was already prominent in Parisian avant-garde circles. As in the case of Jarry, it has been asked whether or not Apollinaire took Rousseau seriously: a question raised because of Apollinaire's high-spirited sense of humor. It has been alleged that "he cultivated Rousseau with so much passion and seeming sincerity that in the end he fell prey to the obsessive charm of his own hoax." There is, however, no reason to doubt the genuineness of his admiration for Rousseau's painting, which Apollinaire made very clear in the issue of *Soirées de Paris* devoted to Rousseau (published in 1914). Nevertheless, his sincerity was for many years questioned by certain of Apollinaire's narrow-minded contemporaries who were skeptical about the value of Rousseau's art and projected their own skepticism onto whatever they could not understand. It is simply that they did not share the intuitive insight which led Apollinaire and a number of avant-garde artists such as Picasso to love Rousseau's painting as soon as they were exposed to it. And since such an intuitive attraction cannot be explained logically—at best, reasons for it can be guessed in retrospect—they began to suspect that public interest in Rousseau was due to some planned hoax or swindle, and thus looked about for people to blame as the responsible parties. That this theory lasted for so long is partly due to the fact that Rousseau's own attitude encouraged it.

The more closely we scrutinize Rousseau's life in the period following his meeting with Apollinaire, when he was seeing artists and writers regularly, the less we can pin down his character—although we have much more information to go on than we had for his earlier life. He does not seem to be trying to fool anyone, nor does he seem to be fooled. Rather, it seems that confronted with so new and different a set of friends and admirers, he was mainly concerned with holding his own and being accepted as an equal. He was acutely conscious of the fundamental differences between himself and the others—the young Cubist painters, Picasso and Braque, and the poets surrounding them; the Baroness of Oettingen (alias Roch Grey), an intelligent and wealthy woman who was genuinely interested in him; and Ambroise Vollard, the most influential art dealer in Paris, who was now buying his painting. All these people were less concerned with gaining his friendship than he was with gaining their respect, and it was doubtless to impress them that he assumed a mask. For in these same years he remained very much the Père Rousseau of his own quarter, who painted his neighbor, the greengrocer Juniet, seated in his light carriage with his wife and children. Juniet had just bought a superb dapple-gray horse of which he was very proud, and it had been agreed that Rousseau would paint a group portrait, including the horse. A photograph was taken of the group *(fig. 137)*, which Rousseau used as his model; he may also have recalled that Gérôme had painted a family in an Egyptian chariot. This took place in 1908 when Cubism was the talk of the town. It is not really surprising, under the circumstances, that Rousseau never discussed painting with Apollinaire and the Cubists. He was sufficiently sensitive to realize that his problems were utterly different from theirs. They did not speak the same language. When André Salmon, one day in the Louvre, asked which painting impressed him most, he could not have answered any differently than he did: "You see, there are so many you can't remember all the names!" It is rather beside the point, in such a connection, to ask whether Rousseau actually had a good memory for names. The truth is, he did not wish to answer—he gave an answer he could hide behind, an anodyne reply which, in conjunction with his gentleness of personality, served as a mask.

Rousseau was with Apollinaire and the Cubists often enough, but he was not really *of* them. One example should suffice. The twentieth century was being heralded in the works of the Cubists by a radically new plastic conception, but in Rousseau's paintings its most obvious signs of progress were recorded as though through the eyes of a child. With genuine feeling, he drew the early biplanes in full flight *(fig. 120)*, just as decades earlier he had put a balloon in his self-portrait *(colorplate, page 31)*. Similarly, he faithfully reproduced the dirigible "Patrie" which had flown over the military parade on July 14, 1907, not missing a detail: the fins and ailerons, the cabin just where it actually was, the tricolor streaming in the breeze *(figs. 118 and 119)*. The casual viewer might suppose this was a fairly stereotyped early airship, but not at all: Rousseau carefully noticed the distinctive features of the "Patrie," including its differences from the "Lebaudy" of a few years earlier. Rousseau reacted to the epoch in his own way, mirroring it in his works. His famous *The Football Players (colorplate, page 111)*, executed in 1908, reflects the beginning of this game's vogue in France. But to whom could he have confided his actual plastic concerns? Which of the avant-garde writers or artists would have listened to him without smiling? He had no choice but to put on a mask of bland benevolence when he was with them, sustained by confidence in his ability, and radiating genuine good will and friendliness.

One day, in his lawyer's office, he made a telephone call. "Suddenly I heard him shouting," Maître Guilhermet tells us. "Surprised, I asked him why he was speaking so loudly, and he replied, 'The people I'm talking to are so far away.'" Rousseau was trying so hard to appear naïve that he occasionally overacted the part. This was a form of self-defense, but the naïveté with which he approached the part made him seem much more naïve than he really was—hence, the distorted image that those who knew him passed on to us. We should not find this so hard to understand. The more exactly observed the recorded impression of him, the more certain we can be that we are dealing with an aspect of Rousseau which he molded according to the circumstances of the moment, to impress the observer of that moment. What motivated him was not, however, a desire to give a false impression. His play acting had a deeper and purer cause: it was simply his fate to be ambiguous to everyone but himself. No one ever knew him as an integral personality. Rousseau the artist was a mystery to his closest neighbors, the people who saw him most, and Rousseau the man completely eluded the intellectuals who wrote and published their recollections of him. Fully half of Rousseau remained in shadow at all times, like the dark side of the moon—a perfect situation to inspire contradictory anecdotes.

One day Apollinaire and his friends informed Rousseau that Dujardin-Baumetz, superintendent of the Beaux-Arts, was going to call on him at his studio. A reception was organized, and one of them disguised himself as "Monsieur le Ministre," with the rosette of the Légion d'honneur in his lapel. He made a speech, the concierge's daughter presented him with a bouquet of flowers, Apollinaire gave a running commentary on the paintings very glibly and skillfully, while the others had a hard time keeping a straight face. Rousseau was radiantly happy. Then the whole company, including "Monsieur le Ministre," went for a drink to a nearby café. One of those present assures us that Rousseau "died convinced that Dujardin-Baumetz had paid him an official visit." Was he really convinced?

On another occasion he was handed an invitation to a party being given by the President of the Republic. When he came back, he told a long story: the guards had refused to admit him, he had insisted, and the President in person had come out and, patting him on the shoulder, said, "It's a pity, Rousseau, that you're in everyday clothes. You see, everybody is in evening dress. Come back some other time." But did he ever really go to the Elysée?

In my opinion, one passage in Apollinaire's essay on Rousseau provides an answer to such questions, not flatly but indirectly. The truth slips into the poet's testimony, even as the legend is being encouraged:

"Few artists have been more jeered at in their lifetimes than the Douanier, and few men faced with greater calm the scoffing and abuse that was showered upon him. This courteous old man always kept an even temper, and by a fortunate trait of character, interpreted the mockery as a sign of interest—a sign that even the most ill-disposed persons were, so to speak, obliged to take interest in his works. Needless to say, his serenity was nothing but pride. The Douanier was perfectly aware of his own powers."

These words may supply the key that we are seeking: Rousseau's serenity was nothing but pride; awareness of his own powers. These few lines are the only ones capable of helping us to understand Rousseau's behavior at the memorable banquet held in his honor in Picasso's studio, and at the no less memorable "family and artistic" evenings Rousseau organized in his own home.

The Banquet at Picasso's Studio

In November 1908, when he was rummaging around in Père Soulié's junkshop, Picasso came across a large portrait of a woman by Rousseau *(fig. 26)*. "You'll be able to use the frame," Soulié is reported to have said to him, letting him have the work for five francs (roughly, the price of admission to a cinema today). In this same period Père Soulié was buying Picasso's drawings at one franc apiece. Thus the young artist was able to afford a Rousseau, and he has kept the painting to this day. To celebrate the purchase he held a banquet in honor of Rousseau in his studio in the Bateau-Lavoir, the famous wooden structure in the Rue Ravignan, legendary ever since as one of the cradles of modern art.

We have several different accounts of the banquet. Fernande Olivier (who was then living with Picasso), Maurice Raynal, and Gertrude Stein have all described the evening in detail, each according to his best recollection. Despite variations, however, the exuberant atmosphere of life in Montmartre in those days comes through vividly, and the Rousseau banquet strikes us as characteristic of the "good old days" which came to an end in 1914.

The evening began in a café near the Bateau-Lavoir. The numerous guests met there and had their first drinks. Then the whole crowd trooped up to Picasso's studio. Two adjoining studios were borrowed to serve as cloakrooms. Among those present were Georges Braque, Marie Laurencin, Guillaume Apollinaire, Max Jacob, Gertrude Stein, André Salmon, Maurice Raynal, many pretty women, and even—we are told—"three art collectors who came from New York, Hamburg, and San Francisco, almost for the sole purpose of attending the banquet." The guests took their places at a long table set on trestles; garlands of Chinese lanterns illuminated the studio. Hung on the wall was the new Rousseau painting, draped in bunting with a banner on which was printed "Honneur à Rousseau!"

"In the midst of the tumult," Maurice Raynal writes, "three discreet knocks were heard at the door, and all the noise stopped. In the ensuing silence, the door opened, and there stood the Douanier, wearing a soft felt hat, carrying a stick in his left hand, and a violin under his right arm . . . . Rousseau can scarcely ever have made a more touching picture. He looked about, was delighted with the Chinese lanterns, and his face brightened."

Now the banquet could begin, but the dinner which had been ordered did not come. After waiting around a couple of hours, Picasso suddenly remembered that he had given the caterer the wrong date. Then the real excitement started. Everybody ran out to get food. "Since the host had in reserve about fifty worthwhile bottles, nobody complained at the delay. Beginning with the tins of sardines the greatest happiness prevailed, and then came the speeches and songs.

Banks of the Oise, about 1905

The Douanier took out his violin, a kind of child's violin, and played one of his compositions, entitled *Clochettes*. Other tunes followed, and soon there was talk of dancing. The Douanier played a waltz of his own, *Clémence*. Rousseau began to get restless, the more so because hot wax was dripping on his head from one of the paper lanterns. He was more comfortable moving about, singing his entire repertory." That was Raynal's version, whereas according to Fernande Olivier the wax gradually formed a great caul over Rousseau's head, and he gently went to sleep where he sat, while the party all around him got wilder and wilder. "At one end of the table," Maurice Raynal says, "Guillaume Apollinaire had seized the opportunity to answer letters he had put off for two months, and improvised a poem which he recited on the spot:

Tu te souviens, Rousseau, du paysage astèque,
Des forêts où poussaient la mangue et l'ananas,
Des singes répandant tout le sang des pastèques
Et du blond empereur qu'on fusilla là-bas.

Les tableaux que tu peins, tu les vis au Mexique:
Un soleil rouge ornait le front des bananiers
Et valeureux soldat, tu troquas ta tunique
Contre le dolman bleu des braves douaniers.

Le malheur s'acharna contre ta progéniture,
Tu perdis tes enfants et tes femmes aussi
Et te remaria avecque la peinture
Pour faire les tableaux, enfants de ton esprit.

Nous sommes réunis pour célébrer ta gloire,
Ces vins qu'en ton honneur nous verse Picasso,
Buvons-les donc, puisque c'est l'heure de les boire
En criant tous en chœur: "Vive! Vive Rousseau!"

Peintre glorieux de l'alme République,
Ton nom est le drapeau des fiers Indépendants
Et dans le marbre blanc, issu du Pentélique,
On sculptera ta face, orgueil de notre temps.

Or sus! que l'on se lève et qu'on choque les verres
Et que renaisse ici la française gaieté;
Arrière noirs soucis, fuyez ô fronts sévères,
Je bois à mon Rousseau, je bois à sa santé!

[You remember, Rousseau, the Aztec landscape
Of forests where mango and pineapple grow,
Where monkeys spill the watermelons' blood,
Way out there where the blond emperor was shot.

The scenes you paint, you saw them in Mexico:
A red sun decorated the brows of the banana trees,
Valiant soldier, you swapped your tunic
For the custom officer's blue jacket.

Misfortune pursued your offspring,
You lost your children and your wives as well,
So you married again, to painting now,
Making pictures, the children of your mind.

We are gathered to celebrate your fame,
And so let us drink the wine Picasso is pouring
To honor you, for it is time to drink it
Crying all in chorus, "Long live! Long live Rousseau!"

Glorious painter of our dear Republic
Your name is the flag of the proud Indépendants,
And it is in white marble, wrested from the Pentelic,
That your features will be sculptured, pride of our age.

Come on! Let us rise and let us clink glasses,
And let French gaiety be reborn here;
Away dull cares, let's see no furrowed brows,
I drink to my Rousseau, I drink to his health!]

We can imagine what the Douanier must have felt. The words of tribute must have been sweet to his ears. It has been alleged that the banquet in his honor was merely another practical joke, but it is hard to believe. In any case, even if some of the guests repressed a smile, there was the Douanier, proudly seated on a "throne made of a chair placed on top of a packing crate" which Picasso had improvised for him. It was Rousseau's moment of consecration.

Evenings at Rousseau's Studio

Decidedly, during this man's lifetime, his destiny as an artist was consummated on some plane other than that of reality, on some "other side" of reality which is not dream, but is not reality either. It was there that the Douanier felt that his reputation was being made—and it was only there, in the realm of the uncertain, that his success was tangible.

He took the appearance of fame, which was his lot, for the real thing, and acted accordingly. No longer was there so rigid a set of barriers between his life in the Plaisance quarter and his relations outside it. The parties he began to give in his studio show this. No longer the eccentric of his quarter, the poor crackpot, he now became Monsieur Rousseau, professor at the Ecole Philotechnique, an artist well known in Paris—the people who came to his parties were enough to prove this. The baker's wife in her Sunday best, the grocer, the dairyman, and their sons and daughters now mingled with such figures of the Paris avant garde as Apollinaire, Picasso, Delaunay, Max Jacob, Georges Duhamel, André Salmon, Braque, and Maître Guilhermet. Here they shook hands, perhaps for the first time in their lives, with foreigners like the American Max Weber and the Germans Wilhelm Uhde and Adolphe Basler. Rousseau himself drew up programs for these incredible evenings, had them hectographed in red, and sent them to his friends. And what programs!

Evening of November 14, 1908
given by M. Henri Rousseau in his Studio
2-bis rue Perrel
ORCHESTRA

"Ave Maria"	Gounod
"La Marche des Pierrots"	Bosc
"Reginette"	Bosc
"Babillage"	Gillot
"Les Deux Frères"	Rousseau
"The Marseillaise"	

Madame Fister in her repertory
Mademoiselle Jeanne
Monsieur Rousseau (violin solo) in his works and creations

This touching parody of the sort of party still current early in the century culminated in a sentence which conveys the host's zeal: "The Stage is put at the disposal of all the guests."

In a later program, the Douanier, now a more accomplished host, changes his formula: "M. Henri Rousseau asks his numerous guests kindly to give their

Liberty Inviting the Artists to Exhibit at the 22nd Salon des Indépendants, 1906

valuable assistance to this evening—Songs and Recitations." And, like the true republican he was, he never omitted "The Marseillaise" from the programs.

After the musical part, he served apples and cookies to the children and wine to the adults, genuinely pleased to have company. Insensitive as usual to the mockeries of practical jokers (there were always some among his guests), he didn't care how big the parties became. At the end of an invitation of July 1909 he added a postscript: "Please inform your friends." The door of his studio was open to everyone, to all his admirers. Henri Rousseau held open house.

In earlier years, when he had no friends, he occasionally pasted the same press cutting about himself twice in his scrapbook. This was not because he was absent-minded, but because he hoped to impress possible visitors with the number of mentions of him in the newspapers. Now the clippings were pasted in more hastily, and we can also see that his life no longer revolved about the Salon des Indépendants. In addition to the old scrapbook on which he had written in a careful hand, "Notices de divers Jours," he now kept a notebook in which he entered his sales. One column contained the names of the paintings sold, another the prices.

The Douanier's life had changed. As we have seen, he began to sell fairly regularly in 1907. The initials "M. B.," discreetly printed in the catalogue of the Indépendants, are those of M. Joseph Brummer, owner of the paintings exhibited. This young art dealer, who later settled in New York City, was interested in the Douanier, bought his canvases, and became one of his friends. Rousseau painted a portrait of him, which was exhibited at the Salon des Indépendants in 1909 (*fig. 134*). By then he had become a close friend of Wilhelm Uhde as well, the most clear-sighted collector of his time, and a great admirer of Rousseau. It was he who in 1908 organized the first and only one-man show the Douanier had during his lifetime. It was, however, another shabby trick played on him by fate.

A furniture dealer in the Rue Notre-Dame-des-Champs asked Uhde to decorate the walls of his store with a few paintings. Uhde, full of enthusiasm, addressed himself to Rousseau and set about preparing a full-fledged exhibition. The Douanier transported his paintings in a handcart. Invitations were sent out. On opening day, Uhde and Rousseau were there, eager to see how the public would react, but nobody came. Only later did Uhde notice that he had forgotten to put down the address of the store on the invitations.

The Douanier, however, would never let himself be discouraged. He had become more self-confident and when the need arose could defend himself. Having read an article which attributed to him a grotesque painting—it showed the Tsar and Kaiser Wilhelm II naked and had been removed from the Salon des Indépendants in 1908 at the request of the police—Rousseau did not hesitate to write to the author, and in his scrapbook noted next to the clipping: "One error that has been corrected!" He had endured mockery for years, but he was not going to let anyone make fun of him under false pretenses.

He was also emboldened by his sales. He aimed high: he called on one of the greatest art dealers in Paris. "One morning," writes Vollard, "a man came in, whom I took to be a messenger. Untying a parcel he had under his arm, he produced two or three small canvases. 'I am a painter,' he said. Nor did he confine himself to painting. He told me that he was teaching a course in music. 'My pupils,' was the rather grand phrase he used for a few young clerks in the Plaisance quarter where he lived."

Vollard's tone is patronizing and ironical. His recollections are the only clues we possess as to how the old painter behaved toward the great powers of his day. With Vollard, we can see, he exhibited a good deal of cunning, reciting his verses and telling a good many ghost stories—in short, he played the part of a simpleton. One day he told Vollard about a ghost who used to tease him when he worked for the toll service, sticking out his tongue and thumbing his nose at him. When Vollard asked why he was so sure it was a ghost, Rousseau replied: "Monsieur Apollinaire said so."

For a long time this image of a very naïve Rousseau was taken at face value. Vollard himself speaks of him as *la complaisance en personne*—smugness personified. But going to the opposite extreme, counter to the legendary image, I am tempted to think that in his relations with the great art dealer, Rousseau was anything but sincere.

In 1909 and 1910 Vollard was his best customer. In 1910 Rousseau sold him 2,150 gold francs' worth of paintings; this was a considerable sum at the time. But in many of these paintings he compromised on quality—not in our eyes, for we have no prejudice against rapid brush strokes, but in his own eyes, for he himself respected only the most carefully finished work. As he said in a letter to Apollinaire, he was working "on commission." And since there was some haggling about prices, he painted fast: he would be rather more conscientious when he did not feel he was being taken advantage of. Even according to the legend, Rousseau filled commissions more diligently the more they paid. This was allegedly the case with the portrait of a child entitled *Baby's Party* (also called *Child with Punch, colorplate, page 73*) which he sold for 300 francs—a price he never obtained again for a painting of these dimensions.

It is interesting to note Rousseau's reactions whenever he is dealing with money. Do they merely indicate that he had been extremely poor for much of his life? I think that we know very little about this aspect of his character. It has only recently been discovered that long before his trial he had been in trouble for having signed a note he had been unable to meet. On the other hand, we know that with the 1,000 francs he got from Sauvaget, he bought a bond issued by the municipality of Paris, acting in the sensible, provident manner we expect of a petty bourgeois. Furthermore, in his letters to Apollinaire he repeatedly complains about a distressing shortage of funds, which compels him to ask for advances on the sum the poet owes him for his portrait, although there was no reason for his poverty at the time the letters were written—unless, that is, he was investing the sums he got from Vollard and other purchasers. Was it really poverty that made Rousseau write Apollinaire in April 1909: 91

"... I am very hard up, tonight I have only 15 centimes for supper. I hope you will be good enough to advance me some money for the work on your portrait. Several persons have asked me how much you are going to pay me for it, and I told them 300 francs, and they thought it was not expensive. It's true that I am making that price for a friend." Some time later he wrote: "Today I have only a few sous to live on until next week. I don't know how I will manage; I must also pay 35 francs for a suit I need, for I have nothing decent, and you know I must go out. My shoes, too, are looking pretty seedy. Remember that for a year I have had more losses than anything else." Finally, in July he wrote: "On August 5 I must pay my wine bill. You see it's serious. In all, it would come to 63 francs. If you are absolutely unable to send me that much, try to give me 40 francs. You'd spare me a lot of trouble for I don't want my bill to be protested. I'd lose my credit, which I need. I am counting on you, my dear friend."

What a strange man he was! The same series of letters, all motivated by the portrait of Apollinaire and "his Muse," on which he was then working, shows how much he had set his heart on the portrait. It is also clear that he attached great importance to Apollinaire's friendship: on several occasions, in order to make sure that the poet could attend his evenings, he asked him to pick the day that suited him best before sending out invitations. As for the portrait, he made a second version of it after the first had been exhibited, because he had painted gillyflowers in the foreground instead of sweet williams (œillets de poète), symbolically more appropriate to poetry. But at the same time, though usually generous, he worried when Apollinaire fell behind in his payments.

Here we are at a loss to understand Rousseau. We have tried to remove the mask whenever it became apparent, but here the mask merges with the features beneath it. Psychologically, the Douanier was a very complex man. We may recall what Maître Guilhermet said when, explaining his client's naïveté to the jury, he summed up his personal impressions in the statement: "Rousseau has been a riddle to me." Robert Delaunay, too, felt that an impassable gulf separated Rousseau from his friends. "I saw a lot of Rousseau," he writes. "We were friends, and I was above all attracted by his art. But the man was such a mystery to me, he was so secretive, that I could not be sure whether he was really having a hard time or not."

Delaunay was not mistaken. Seen from the outside, the Douanier's fate seemed harsh. Anyone else in his place would have been miserable. Rousseau, however, lived happily through everything, because he had managed to arrange his life according to a principle rather like those nests of Chinese boxes—every time we think we have reached the last one, there is still another within that one. Can we ever get to the bottom of such a life?

In all his letters concerning the portrait of Apollinaire, Rousseau showed himself busy, remarkably full of vitality for a man of sixty-four. Although he painted a great deal, he often went out. Among other activities, he still gave

Still Life with Coffeepot, 1907

lessons in students' homes at a considerable distance from his quarter and made "his orchestra study hard" for the "family and artistic evenings" he enjoyed so much. Now and then he went to the country not far from Paris for a couple of days, to paint from nature the little landscapes which gave him so much pleasure. And he saw people, quite ordinary, obscure people whom, from time to time, he asked Apollinaire to help. One was out of a job, another was a painter whom he recommended. He did not hesitate to write to Félix Fénéon, director of the Galerie Bernheim-Jeune, urging him to buy paintings by one of his friends, and giving his opinion. After observing that they were "of excellent worksmanship," he added, "At the same time, if your firm were willing to take some of my works, which you are certainly familiar with, I should be happy to sell you one or more of them." The same day, November 23, 1908, he used the word "certainly" again in a letter addressed to Apollinaire, arranging a sitting. "The painting is liked a great deal," he writes. "Therefore we mustn't put it off any longer. I want to go right ahead and paint a lovely composition which, certainly, will produce a sensation."

The portrait in question (*colorplate, page 131*), on which the Douanier worked for several months, was finally exhibited at the Salon des Indépendants in 1909. Did it cause a sensation? Doubtless Apollinaire had more to say about it than anyone else. This is what he said:

"... The whole press is amused by my portrait, which was reproduced in *Comœdia*.

"The whole press was unanimous in its conclusions, namely, that this portrait does not resemble me in the slightest. Some found it touching, others verging on the grotesque, but as for resemblance, everybody agreed that there is none. This surprised me. If it didn't resemble me, how did it come about that I was recognized? I had asked the Douanier not to mention my name; had he broken his word? But after consulting the catalogue of the exhibition I had to pay tribute to his good faith, for it bore only this inscription: 'The Muse Inspiring the Poet.'

"On the other hand, neither the Douanier nor myself frequented editorial offices, and we were acquainted with few journalists.

"At that time they did not pay much attention to me, nor do they even today; as for him, they ignored him completely. Under the circumstances, how could they recognize me sufficiently to discover that the portrait does not look like me? Why, despite the title given in the catalogue, did all the newspapers refer to the painting as *La Muse d'Apollinaire* or *Apollinaire et sa Muse* or else *Le Poète Guillaume Apollinaire inspiré par la Muse?*

"I tend to believe that the portrait is so striking and original a likeness that against their will they were dazzled. Painting is the most religious art. In 1909 we witnessed a phenomenon of collective suggestion of the kind that gives rise to the purest religions. It was a sublime adventure, and I am glad I went through it. My face has served a unique experiment, which I shall never forget."

The portrait earned Rousseau a highly laudatory review from Arsène Alexandre. "Only our good Douanier Rousseau could be incapable of intending what he has done," the critic wrote. "Had he set out to achieve these touching allegories, this form, and these colors according to some coldly calculated system, he would be the most dangerous of men, when in fact he is the most sincere and candid. Were they not so expensive, one would like to own some of his works, not to hang on the wall, for they would exercise a dangerous fascination on our minds, but only to look at them from time to time when we feel the need to be reminded of what sincerity is. If he possessed what he completely lacks, namely, science, and could at the same time preserve his freshness of conception, Rousseau would be the Paolo Uccello of our century."

A little later, Arsène Alexandre called on Rousseau in his studio. When he reported his talk with the artist, he mentioned the Jardin des Plantes instead of Mexico, and Apollinaire dismissed this substitution as whimsical. What the Douanier had said was: "When I enter those hothouses and I see these strange plants from faraway countries, I have the impression that I am walking into a dream."

That was the truth; but it was too blinding to be looked at squarely. The Douanier's exotic landscapes seemed so consistent with this impressive alibi—the journey to Mexico—that the truth was felt as an unwelcome intrusion.

Viewers were reminded of the tropics the following year, in 1910, when Rousseau exhibited at the Indépendants the large painting entitled *The Dream* (*colorplate, page 133*). The following poem was attached to the frame:

> *Yadwigha dans un beau rêve*
> *S'étant endormie doucement*
> *Entendait les sons d'une musette*
> *Dont jouait un charmeur bien pensant.*
> *Pendant que la lune reflète*
> *Sur les fleuves, les arbres verdoyants,*
> *Les fauves serpents prêtent l'oreille*
> *Aux air gais de l'instrument.*

> [Yadwigha, peacefully asleep,
> Enjoys a lovely dream:
> She hears a kind snake charmer
> Playing upon his reed.
> On stream and foliage glisten
> The silvery beams of the moon;
> And savage serpents listen
> To the gay, entrancing tune.]

Rousseau was worried about how the painting would be received. "I learned from Picasso that you review paintings for the *Intransigeant*," he wrote to

95

Apollinaire on the eve of the opening. "I think that you will display your literary talent and avenge me for the insults and snubs I have been subjected to." Apollinaire devoted a long passage to Rousseau in his column, conveying his sincere admiration. It begins with a description of the painting: "On an 1850-style sofa a nude woman lies asleep. Around her is tropical vegetation peopled by monkeys and birds of paradise; a lion and a lioness go by quietly, and a Negro—a mysterious personage—is playing a flute." He concludes in a tone of conviction: "That the painting emanates beauty, is incontestable . . . . I think that this year no one will dare to laugh. . . . Ask painters what they think. They are unanimous: they all admire it. They admire everything about it, even the Louis-Philippe sofa swallowed up in the virgin forest, and they are right."

Nevertheless, the red sofa greatly baffled other critics. Thereupon, the Douanier wrote one of them in his best style to explain his painting. "This woman sleeping on the sofa," he wrote to André Dupont, "dreams that she is transported into the middle of this forest, hearing the notes of the charmer's pipe. This gives the motive for the sofa being in the picture."

While Rousseau was busy justifying his painting's strange subject, a no less strange addition was being made to his biography, based on the picture. The nude Yadwigha, shown asleep on the red sofa (which everyone who had ever visited Rousseau's studio recognized), became, in contemporary accounts, the woman Rousseau had loved in his youth, a foreigner—sometimes Russian, sometimes Polish, sometimes described as a schoolteacher. Between this tale and that of the romantic journey to Mexico, the Douanier's past was taking on legendary proportions in his own lifetime, inspired by the mysterious lighting of the painting, and fed also by his life and personality. For now, at the age of sixty-five, Rousseau fell in love again. He was very much in love and very unhappy. Léonie, the woman he loved, a widow of fifty-four, refused him, and her parents were adamantly against the marriage. Every night he stood outside the store where Léonie worked as a saleslady, hoping to soften her heart. As a last resource, he asked his friends Vollard and Apollinaire to give him written recommendations, testifying to his talent and his honesty. There was nothing he was not prepared to do for Léonie. In 1909 he drew up a will in her favor, as follows:

"To Mlle Eugénie-Léonie V. . . ., widow of M. Auguste V. . . ., her first husband (wife of M. Henri Rousseau, artist-painter, her second husband), my dearest friend, to whom I owe great and eternal gratitude, I herewith bequeath all that I possess, furniture, jewelry, money, paintings. Moreover, I authorize her to demand a royalty of 20% on all sales to art dealers and other purchasers. My dear Léonie will be good enough to give half of whatever sums are realized to my daughter, Julia Rousseau, married name Bernard, residing at Angers, département of Maine-et-Loire."

The will, however, was never signed or dated, for Léonie refused to marry him. Shortly before his death he wrote her a letter which makes the whole situation quite clear. At the top of the first page Rousseau drew a pansy (*une*

The Snake Charmer, 1907

pensée). "All my thoughts *[pensées]* are for you," he wrote under the flower, and with a heavy heart began the letter:

Saturday evening, August 19, 1910

My beloved Léonie,

Before turning in, I want to say a few words to you about the remark you made at Vincennes while we were sitting on the bench waiting for the trolley. You said that if I was of no use to you, I served at least as your buffoon ..."

The indignant tone Rousseau's friends took when they spoke of Léonie is understandable, as was their affection for the old painter and their desire to comfort him. One day Roch Grey gave him a ring, suggesting that he should give it to his beloved. Léonie accepted it, just as she had accepted other gifts, but it did not change her attitude.

In those days Rousseau often went to call on Roch Grey. He confided in her. Watching him suffer, she wondered sadly "how he could reconcile his rare, precious fondness for dream plants and exotic animals with his passion for a nasty, unfeeling shopgirl." One day when Roch Grey was about to go on a trip, Rousseau came to say goodbye to her. From her balcony she watched him leave. "He walked fast, a little stooped, seeming very old and very tiny in the emptiness of the interminable boulevard."

That was the last time she saw the Douanier. When she got back to Paris, she learned that he had died.

Thanks to Robert Delaunay we know the circumstances of his death—he witnessed the Douanier's last days. As was his habit, Delaunay went to see him at his studio. Rousseau complained of a pain in the leg. "Apparently he had hurt it, somehow. We talked about the paintings I had brought to show him, but I saw that he was dejected and his mind wasn't on what we were talking about. I had a sort of foreboding and called back at the studio a few days later. One of his neighbors, a woman, told me that he was in the hospital, very sick. I rushed there. Rousseau was close to death. He could scarcely recognize me, and while he was keeping my hands in his, squeezing them, I was desperately trying to think what I could do. It occurred to me that the woman he loved would be the best thing for him at a time like this. So I went to where she lived, in the Rue du Temple, and begged her to go and see him the next day, Sunday I explained where the hospital was, and that he would not live much longer. She never came, and Rousseau died in despair, with only M. Queval, his friend and landlord, and Mme Queval at his side."

Rousseau died on September 2, 1910, at the Hôpital Necker in Paris. Though the cause of death was gangrene (the leg had become infected), the hospital diagnosed him as an "alcoholic"—the last of so many ironical twists and turns in his strange life.

At that very moment, the Italian painter Ardengo Soffici, in the avant-garde magazine *La Voce*, was publishing the only article entirely devoted to

Rousseau's painting since the one published in the *Mercure de France* in 1895. The article was actually on press when Soffici learned of the Douanier's death.

Rousseau's funeral was held on September 4. Seven persons followed the hearse; among them was Paul Signac, president and founder of the Société des Artistes Indépendants. One year later Delaunay and Queval raised the money to have his remains transferred from the pauper's grave to a thirty-year plot in the cemetery of Bagneux. Apollinaire wrote in chalk a poem-epitaph on the tombstone, which was later chiseled into the stone by Brancusi and the painter Ortiz de Zarate. The poet's handwriting was faithfully reproduced. In 1942, thanks to the Association des Amis de Rousseau, the thirty-year plot was secured in perpetuity, and a few years later, in 1947, the remains were moved to Laval. The Douanier now rests in a public park in the town where he was born. A medallion by his faithful friend, Armand Queval, by trade a caster in metals, decorates his tomb, on which is engraved Apollinaire's epitaph:

Gentil Rousseau tu nous entends
Nous te saluons
Delaunay sa femme Monsieur Queval et moi
Laisse passer nos bagages à la porte du ciel
Nous t'apporterons des pinceaux des couleurs des toiles
Afin que tes loisirs sacrés dans la lumière réelle
Tu les consacres à peindre comme tu tiras mon portrait
Face aux étoiles.

[Gentle Rousseau you can hear us
We salute you
Delaunay his wife Monsieur Queval and myself
Let our luggage pass duty-free through the gate of heaven
We are bringing you brushes paints and canvas
That you may spend your sacred leisure hours
Painting in the light of truth eternal
As you once painted my portrait
Facing the stars.]

Work

Rousseau's work raises almost as many questions as his life. Though produced relatively recently—between 1885 and 1910—it presents problems that we expect to find when dealing with some long-forgotten artist of the distant past. There the paintings are, amazing but baffling, assimilable as a whole, but well-nigh impossible to reconstruct in terms of detailed development. What was the origin of his art? What were its intentions? In what direction does it point? When it comes to answering such fundamental questions, our traditional aesthetic concepts are put to heavy strain. Customary art-history assumptions simply do not apply here. Rousseau remains an exceptional artist, easy to admire but resistant to analysis.

Just consider: had Rousseau lived a quarter of a century earlier—had he died in 1885, before a revolutionary salon like the Salon des Indépendants was founded—not a single one of his works would ever have been shown in public. Such few of his works as might have escaped destruction would strike us as remote, as utterly *sui generis*, without the slightest relation to anything else in the art of the nineteenth century. Even so, living when he did and, thanks to the Salon des Indépendants, attaining a certain prestige or notoriety with the art public of his day, Rousseau's painting still strikes us as essentially isolated from the other artistic currents of the period. He is like some lonely island, all trace of whose links with the rest of the archipelago have been blotted out by the sea. We stand outside his art, which seems to have sprung full-blown from his brush, without undergoing any preliminary preparation or development.

The problem, I suspect, is that we have to set aside our traditional expectations and acknowledge that the customary categories of art-history analysis simply do not apply here. Only by taking into account the very particularity, the genuinely exceptional character of Rousseau's art, can we hope to reconstruct

The Repast of the Lion, 1907

its origin and sense. In this connection, two historical features of the later nineteenth century seem especially cogent: the decline of academic art on the one hand, and the decline of the handicrafts on the other. If we are to situate this remarkable artist anywhere, I suggest that it should be at the point where these historical developments intersect.

The decline of academic painting represented a profound break within the very principle of art. The system of interlocking schools and salons—the uniformly taught and practiced conception of painting—was now challenged by a conception of art defined as the free expression of the individual. The founding of the Salon des Indépendants—an annual exhibition without a jury and without prizes—incarnated this challenge. The Impressionists spearheaded the development when they simply refused to roll over and die because the official salon had rejected their works. Only under such propitious circumstances could a painter like Rousseau have found a place to show his paintings—or, indeed, have found anyone willing to accord him the status of artist. At the same time, however, we must recognize that this development in itself does not adequately account for the quality and character of Rousseau's painting. Exhibit with the Impressionists, the Fauves, Cézanne, and others he certainly did—but his attitudes toward art were very different from theirs, just as his paintings were very different from theirs.

In their highly self-conscious break with the academic tradition, these artists searched for new bases on which to build their painting—and did so with an unprecedented degree of individuality. However, for all their dissimilarities, all of them turned back to the history of art for their clues, and it was in every case some phase of that history they drew upon. This was the point on which Rousseau differed radically from the avant-garde painters he exhibited with.

Today—and especially *since* Rousseau—we have become aware that, alongside the old masters and the classical tradition of Western art, there has always existed a certain tradition of "primitive," or "folk," art, which has been elaborated over the centuries rather less ambitiously (culturally speaking) than the former. It is art practiced at the handicraft level, the artistic instinct in its simplest expression. The primitive, or folk, artist follows some previously set pattern, without feeling therefore "pinned down" or "held back," and without feeling compelled to "go beyond" his model. Folk art changes very slowly, almost imperceptibly, and its patterns are endlessly repeated; the folk artist seems unconscious of his power, content to remain a mere craftsman. Most often in the past such artists were anonymous. In the Middle Ages the social distinction between the arts and the crafts was not recognized, and artists were not distinguished from craftsmen.

Then there was a point in the nineteenth century when, with the rise of industrial mass production, these two long-distinct categories of artist and craftsman once again came close together. As handmade articles became rare and expensive, they began to take on the dignity of works of art. It is against the background of this particular sociological development that the exceptional

Merry Jesters, 1906

case of the painter Rousseau begins to make sense. Indeed a primitive, or folk, artist, he was a craftsman whom historical conditions projected into the category of "art" during a particularly crucial phase of its development. At a moment when the most talented painters were loudly demanding recognition of the individual sensibility, and in a city where this particular assault on tradition was being carried farther than anywhere else, art could welcome as an ally even the simplest and least sophisticated instinctual expression. In this perspective, Rousseau symbolizes a turning point in history—and, thanks to his gifts, all our notions of primitive art today derive from his prodigious example. There were primitive painters before him, just as there have been primitive painters since, but it was his example alone—occurring as it did in an especially crucial time and place—that restored this other tradition to our consciousness. He added something unique to the cultural ferment of the late nineteenth century: thanks to him, the doors of art were flung open once and for all. The art of children and madmen no longer falls outside our aesthetic concepts, and no primitive painter ever again need feel awkward at his lack of formal training and general culture. Indeed, what gives Rousseau's painting its special intensity is undoubtedly the fact that—an exception among primitive artists—he rubbed shoulders with artists so unlike himself and was not left to paint away in comparative obscurity.

As has often been told, Rousseau's favorite painter was Bouguereau. And yet, it is noteworthy that he never took one of Bouguereau's paintings for a model, as he took certain works by other academic painters who are less well remembered today. The fact is noteworthy because it helps us to grasp what was fundamentally contradictory in Rousseau's attitude to painting. Actually, it was not Bouguereau's works that impressed Rousseau. What impressed him (though he did not realize it) was Bouguereau's standing and reputation, in a special sense, and this feeling is not to be confused with envy of Bouguereau's fame. What Rousseau wanted was to be recognized in the same terms as Bouguereau—as the painter par excellence, officially so ranked and popularly so respected. What Rousseau desperately aspired to was status—the more so since he was a self-taught artist who found himself plunged into the world of art with a big "A." To his dying day, Rousseau had an inferiority complex on this score, and, as is not unusual in such cases, one of its components was an inborn, ineradicable respect for accepted values. Hence the contradiction: his conscious attitude to art was desperately conformist, and sincerely so, but his sensibility was revolutionary. He was too poorly educated to recognize the inherent contradiction, and so it never really came to trouble him, never gave rise to conflict. He simply lived with it, unaware that his theory of art and his practice of it were running on separate tracks throughout his entire life. This resulted in the characteristic ambiguity we find at every point in his life.

The foregoing throws light as well on the curious lack of development in the successive elaboration of his art. There is no guiding thread, because his ideas, his conscious purposes, were forever at odds with his sensibility. His opinions on art do not shape his means of expression but remain extraneous to the pictures he painted. What we have, instead, is a progressive clarification of his personal idiom, step by step, in the form of a growing ability to bring out the values selected for emphasis.

Actually, nothing could be more natural; it is just the sort of thing we should expect, and the reason we have not succeeded in pinning Rousseau down heretofore is merely that we have expected this highly untypical artist to obey laws of development derived from the study of more typical artists. Rousseau's art has its own kind of development, which we will now take upon ourselves to trace. Precisely because in his painting, his ideas do not involve his sensibility, the latter remains intact, preserving its instinctual force, and as it emerges in the act of painting, it runs counter to his ideas and upsets the painter's conscious intentions. Consequently, in trying to discern Rousseau's development as an artist, we must keep in mind that, unlike most artists worth studying, Rousseau's head and heart never meet and merge in his work. We must get used to the idea that what he undertakes consciously is well-nigh imaginary, and that actually his painting matures without his being aware of it—not against his will, but independently of his conscious control. The rhythm of his development is irregular and unpredictable, and requires a corresponding flexibility in our means of investigation.

The contradiction inherent in Rousseau's art dogs his every step. Whenever he aims at a certain effect, he obtains something else; the success he pursues remains forever beyond his reach. He is the very model of the painter in whom self-knowledge does not exist. When we study his paintings we find, in every case, that what surmounts the contradictions and saves the painting is his infallible pictorial instinct. In every case its intervention is crucial. This is a constant in his art, and, in our experience of the work as a whole, it forces us to conclude that the key to Rousseau's development is to be found in the increasing freedom with which his pictorial instinct is deployed. Let us compare one of the earliest with one of the last paintings—*Carnival Evening (fig. 35)*, dating from 1886, with *The Dream (colorplate, page 133)*, dating from 1910. They were painted almost a quarter of a century apart. Each work realizes the painter's intentions in its own way, and yet at first glance we might say two different painters produced them. Only closer scrutiny reveals the profound identity between the tangled screen of branches against a luminous background in *Carnival Evening* and the tropical vegetation in *The Dream*. The former is, as it were, the skeleton framework of the latter, where the Douanier's pictorial instinct gave itself free rein.

Of course, this is an extreme comparison. However, I think it is only with the help of such examples that we can discern other, far subtler points of reference, which will enable us to study Rousseau's creative process. It must not be supposed that Rousseau's art developed from the one picture to the other during the intervening twenty-three years. On the contrary, Rousseau's art frequently takes surprising turns. But one thing remains constant: Rousseau always turns out something different from his original aims. He wants to be an

23 *Street Scene* (study for *View of Malakoff*), 1908

View of Malakoff, 1908

academic painter. Artistic conventions are a matter of primary importance to him. He is concerned with what is and what is not "done," and yet it is only to the extent that he lets himself go—when he abandons himself to that part of himself which he consciously disavows—that his art becomes more mature.

It is from this angle that we shall try to consider his painting, keeping in mind both the conscious aims he pursued and how he departed from them in the act of painting. The distance between what he intended and what he achieved accounts not only for the highly personal quality of his art, but also provides clues for dating the works.

Usually, our greatest single aid to understanding a painter's early period is to study the influences he was subjected to before his own style took shape. This is one of our classic means of investigation. We follow the itinerary of the artist as he looks about him for points of support. His choices are indicative of his personality, they disclose the direction he is taking and foreshadow the forms he will eventually develop. But the usual methods simply do not work in the case of Rousseau. The contradiction inherent in his art alters the very concept of influences in many-faceted and important ways. Our whole understanding of Rousseau's art depends largely on the answer we give to this simple question: Just what were the influences that worked on him?

At first glance we would be inclined to say that surely there could have been no influences at all—rarely has there been an art so recognizably *sui generis*. And this is true. From the plastic point of view, Rousseau's formal expression owes nothing to anyone else. This was the domain where instinct conquered forcibly, though Rousseau struggled against it—and, as we have said, the extent to which this artist's instinct gained the upper hand is the measure of the evolution of his painting. In short, the originality of the forms is accidental, and hence they resist, by their very nature, all preconceived ideas. Influence, however, whether conscious or unconscious, is something voluntary. We speak of being subjected to influences, but the passive in this case is an illusion: we choose the influences we subject ourselves to, guided by some more or less obscure desire to identify ourselves with a chosen model. And is not desire the most faithful mirror of the man?

Actually, when we turn our question around and subdivide it, it does apply to Rousseau. In the case of other painters, we speak of influences in the formal sense; in the case of Rousseau, we discover influences in his painting only with respect to content. And here we are due for some surprises.

The moment this point has been settled—the moment we recognize in what sense we may properly speak of influences with regard to Rousseau—we realize that both his first and his last painting reflect influences. Throughout his life he felt the need to follow a pattern, thus proving that the handicraft spirit was more deeply implanted in him than pride in the creative imagination. Here lies the boundary line separating art from so-called folk art: on the one hand, we have forms continually renewed by the creative imagination; on the other, a number of schematic elements which serve as starting points for the man who merely wishes to leave his imprint on things. On the one hand, we have the artist who imperiously asserts his individuality; on the other, the craftsman who is continually looking for a model. And between the two we have the paradox of Rousseau, who was a craftsman in exercising his faculties, but an artist without being aware of it, as the result of his long labors at the easel. Thus, throughout his career, he moved in two worlds. At the level of his awareness he was in one world, whereas at the level of his ambitions, he was in another. Like the craftsman he was, he could paint the same picture twice, almost without variation—in any case, without attempting to push on and broaden his explorations. He did not suspect that the work of art is unique—just as no one had suspected it during the centuries when painting was formally assigned to a craft status. His attitude was as old as art itself, but at the end of the nineteenth century, in the context of the prevailing aesthetics, it relegated him to the status of craftsman. But Rousseau is irreducible: relegated there, he is not in the right category either, for he was never caught up in the routine of perpetuating stereotypes. On the contrary, he made a conspicuous effort to choose his own models. Throughout his career, his choices in this connection attested to his good taste—they bridged the gulf between what he was and what he aspired to be.

Once we begin to speak of models instead of influences and "points of support" instead of "plastic contributions," we get closer to the nature of Rousseau's art. Incidentally, it is clear that if the influences are merely models, they can appear at any moment and can come from anywhere at all. They serve no more than to disclose Rousseau's state of mind at a given moment in his career.

Unfortunately, the works that have come down to us do not represent the full output of Rousseau's career. We know that by 1895 he had produced more than 200 drawings, but only about a dozen of these are known. Of his twenty-five-year output we have only about 150 paintings and only a few of those which were exhibited at the Salon des Indépendants—that is, the works which he regarded as his most important, the ones he finished with the greatest care and gave himself to most completely. The others—that is, the majority of the paintings known to us—were less important in his eyes. Thus we shall never have complete data on his sources of inspiration. It is interesting to note that the reason for this is not only the destruction of a large part of his work, but also the disappearance of his models, the fact they fell into discredit. Rousseau's sources did not survive the passage of time, and it is only by chance that our knowledge of them is occasionally broadened. The academic painting of the nineteenth century which he admired so much enjoyed a short-lived fame; what has not been dispersed lies unseen in museum cellars. As for others of Rousseau's models—engravings in contemporary magazines, throw-aways, colored lithographs, popular prints—they probably exist, but buried in libraries. Day by day, this world of marginal forms has been moving farther away from us, while Rousseau's painting has been moving closer. Underestimated by their first owners, Rousseau's paintings—those that escaped destruction—have revealed their value and present us with the problems we are trying to solve. Only rarely do we happen to possess all the elements for an exhaustive solution; on the other hand, such rare examples as we do possess cast a great deal of light on Rousseau's creative method. Later on, when we go over his works painting by painting, we shall note various models Rousseau followed and the use he made of them. We will see how he transformed the initial subject, what motives induced him to follow a given pattern, and how he dispensed with patterns altogether, painting almost "on his own" little landscapes with trees—always trees.

Had Rousseau's name not come down to us, but only his paintings, I think we would refer to him, as we refer to anonymous painters of the past, as "the Master of the Trees." No painter has ever been more attracted to foliage, whether stirring tremulously or standing immobile. I am tempted to think that Rousseau became a painter out of love for trees. During the monotonous days when he worked for the Paris octroi, there must always have been one or more trees within view, with the help of which he learned to follow the changes of light, the motions of the wind, and the passage of the seasons. I do not base my opinion merely on the fact that one of his earliest drawings (*fig. 28*) is of a tree. I would go further and suppose that the very first time Rousseau took pencil in hand, it was to draw a tree. In short, I believe that the image of the tree was the matrix of his art, rather than the patterns he followed and the models he chose. The image of the tree takes us to the very heart of his artistic temperament, to the very roots of his sure, sound instinct. The following passage from a description of Laval by Trohel, archivist of that town, may be significant in this connection: "To the east, the new quarters extend in the plain, a bluish tide of roofs from which emerge the slender shapes of the bell towers . . . and the trees, tress, countless trees. Laval is a city of trees, and its inhabitants are great tree lovers. The tiniest garden has its plane tree or its chestnut tree, so that in spring the city twitters like an aviary." This is almost the atmosphere of a painting by Rousseau. In any event, this is Rousseau's pictorial universe, to which he stubbornly kept adding a borrowed visual universe. The space encompassed by his painting ranges from the one to the other, situated between these two extremes: between a sure, sound instinct and superficial structures deriving from an inferiority complex about art. His gradual abandonment of superficial structures is the most striking single feature in his artistic development.

It was his love of trees that gave rise to his intense interest in exotic plants. The lushness and variety of tropical vegetation impressed him deeply and encouraged him to express feelings he would otherwise have repressed or tried to reduce to conventional patterns. In the end, his love of it overcame his inferiority complex. Under the pretext of painting "the Mexico of his youth," and with no special attempt to reproduce the tropical flora in any way, he abandoned

The Football Players, 1908

himself to his creative imagination and began to treat—though very cautiously— the vegetal theme which is the moving force of his art. The lush forests of his last years are the very logical end results of his timid early landscapes. Only when he treats this theme does Rousseau's art rise above its inherent contradictions: the theme is the only straight line discernible in his otherwise meandering progress.

Actually, what complicates and almost confuses our vision of this progress is the peculiar character of his hand. Needless to say, the way his hand worked is nothing but the direct reflection of Rousseau's pictorial consciousness or, more accurately, his lack of it. Incontestably, his hand is a very gifted one. To realize this it is enough to glance at an oil drawing such as that of the *Path in Parc Montsouris (fig. 60)*, which, it is true, is not an early work—but a gift is not something you learn. It exists or does not exist. And when it exists, it quite early takes over the reins of an artist's development. In this connection, however, Rousseau is the exception. He distrusted his gifts. His hand did not abandon itself to the motions that came naturally. His line is meticulous, almost tense, and only a few drawings exhibit the sweeping stroke which signifies freedom. Bold touches alternate with revisons, as instinct keeps drawing back in order to take a longer leap forward. This backward-and-foward movement is observable continuously throughout the twenty-five years of Rousseau's career as an artist. The fact is, Rousseau's hand reacts differently to different subjects. Very much at ease in his treatment of trees and every other kind of vegetation, he is less at ease when problems of perspective are involved, and positively timid and clumsy the moment he deals with the human figure. These subjects seem to have been produced by the artist at different stages of his development: the human figures are the work of a beginning artist, the perspective views that of a maturing artist, and the trees—in fact, all the paintings in which vegetation predominates—the work of a mature artist. The continual shifts in the current of Rousseau's development, shifts determined in each case by the subject, strikingly illustrate the manner in which his inferiority complex affected the creative act. Pictorial instinct went astray in all those instances where pictorial science—academism—was, by definition, triumphant.

Now we are in a position to study Rousseau's painting. Keeping in mind the dominating conflict between instinct and consciousness, his reliance upon deliberately chosen patterns, and the influence of the subject upon his means of expression, we may at last be able to present Rousseau's contribution in an adequate chronological order.

View of the Pont de Sèvres, 1908

First Period: 1885—1890

The first works Rousseau exhibited (in 1885) were two paintings, *Sunset* and *Italian Dance*. All we know about them are their titles. But in the light of the foregoing remarks, it is possible to make some plausible conjectures about them. Rousseau, a native of Brittany who never traveled farther from home than Paris, undertook an Italian subject—just like the academic painters who had won their prix de Rome and who often portrayed Italian scenes. We get a first glimpse of Rousseau's aspirations: from the outset it was the academic art of his time that held his attention and constituted his ideal. According to some writers, there were a few paintings, Impressionist in style, dating from approximately the same period, but to me this seems doubtful. In my opinion, Rousseau made his debut under the auspices of the academic painter Clément; this is a point established by biographical data. The permit to copy paintings in the Louvre, which he obtained in 1884, probably reflects some of Clément's advice. It is therefore natural to suppose that *Italian Dance* declared Rousseau's intention to abide by the rules of academic art.

As for the second painting, *Sunset*, the title alone is indicative of Rousseau's lyrical temperament, which kept manifesting itself throughout his career. This is the other pole of his art, the expression of a sensibility which is at odds with his conscious aspirations.

The form Rousseau's sensibility takes in his early works is disclosed by the painting *Carnival Evening (fig. 35)*, which he exhibited in 1886. This is the earliest of Rousseau's extant works, and it is a capital document from the plastic point of view: analysis of it is the only means available for gaining insight into Rousseau's painting in this period. Analysis will also cast light on Rousseau's way of working.

What strikes us at once in *Carnival Evening* is the picture's perfect balance. All the means of expression, from composition to color, work together to raise the subject to its greatest plastic power. The trees that form a hedgerow of lines against the remote background glow, the immensity of the sky which catches the eye and sends it back to the two human figures situated at the optical center of the painting, the moon and clouds that counterbalance the couple, the little house at the left which serves to break the monotony of the line of trees, the perfect color harmony, and, above all, the special atmosphere conveyed by the whole—there is nothing here to suggest a beginning painter. None of the awkwardness that Rousseau will manifest later appears in this painting. To conclude that Rousseau's approach here is unfathomable was only natural in view of all this, and no one has ever gone a step farther toward an explanation. Some, however, have accounted for this mastery by assuming that Rousseau had done a great deal of work before. But if this were so, why does he not display the same mastery in many later paintings? For my part, I believe that we are dealing with a sudden access of mastery, due simply to a combination of plastic circumstances. To confirm this, we need only locate the elements of the painting chronologically, in the context of Rousseau's work as a whole. The moment we have understood the nature of this mastery, we shall see that not only is it compatible with Rousseau's debut as a painter, but that it seems to confirm the very fact that this is, indeed, an early painting.

In setting out to analyze the means of expression in *Carnival Evening*, we must keep one thing in mind, Rousseau's exceptional intuition—his ability to go straight to the point. It manifests itself, to begin with, in his use of color. The choice of tones and color harmonies is spontaneous and right. It was just as spontaneously that the painter's eye chose the center of gravity of the composition—the moon, the two human figures, the relationship between the sky and the trees. The painting cannot fail to be successful, for it raises no problems that cannot be solved intuitively. Nothing in the picture depends on great knowledge of painting; there is no problem of rendering three-dimensional space in successive planes, there is no object in the foreground, and no problems of the relation between space and human figures. In short, there are none of those problems which are traditionally solved according to the unchanging laws of perspective, which the Douanier will soon attack, giving them in each case a solution based solely on his feeling for things. Lacking technical knowledge, he will, down to his last work, reduce perspective to an intuitive element and never grasp its principles. But, nothing if not in earnest, he will prefer as much as possible to let himself be guided, to follow models in surmounting such difficulties when he encounters them. As we shall see later, there are some striking examples in evidence of this. It is, incidentally, thanks to these examples that we can single out one almost insignificant detail in *Carnival Evening* which will provide us with one path through the maze: I refer to the feet of the human figures, which are drawn with sureness, fully in accordance with the requirements of perspective—in this case, the perspective of distant views. This is a plastic solution which Rousseau did not invent. Whereas the mastery of the rest of the painting is accounted for by the absence of problems to trap the beginner, the perfect drawing of this detail can only be accounted for in terms of some model the painter followed. Thus, at the origin of this early landscape by Rousseau there was a model which, judging by the romantic spirit of the subject, may well have been one of the colored lithographs that were still common at the end of the nineteenth century. The forms they used were the kind that could be assimilated intuitively. We shall see that the same subject recurs in another painting, where it involves problems of perspective. By a lucky chance Rousseau was able to avoid them in the earlier painting, though eventually he would have to deal with them.

Walk in the Forest (fig. 41) is the more elaborate version of *Carnival Evening*, but is still very close to the latter. The over-all design is the same in both: trees standing out against the sky, with a human figure taking a walk. But the conception is very different. The purely imaginative quality of *Carnival Evening* has given way to observation. Rousseau tries to define the compositional planes. Playing upon the height of the trees and the volumes of the trunks, he divides the visual space. By forcing the proportions of two trees, one at the right and one at the left, he defines his foreground plane and, motivated by a desire to create an effect of gradually receding depth, he abruptly suggests distance with an imprecise mass of foliage. (Such unexpected solutions, in which his innate lyricism asserts itself, are one of the greatest charms of Rousseau's painting.) When he comes to paint the figure's feet, what does he do? He conceals them. A bush conveniently hides them from view. Rousseau often resorted to this subterfuge, and we can understand why. A foot on the ground defines the space at once. The laws of perspective coldly decree its position. A static detail, the foot creates a difficulty that Rousseau cannot surmount. This is one of his "tics," evidence of the constraint imposed by his conscious aims in art to hold his pictorial instinct prisoner. This sense of constraint, over which Rousseau's instinct is intermittently victorious, is very strong early in his career, but grows weaker toward the end. To repeat ourselves on this score, this is the key to his artistic development. It is not that he ever overcomes the difficulties which account for the constraint; rather, it is that the pressure of instinct gradually renders the artist unconscious of them. They persist unsurmounted, but they lose their importance. An especially clear example is to be found in a painting sold to Vollard—that is, one executed after 1905. It is a third and much freer version of the theme we have just analyzed: *Woman in Red in the Forest* (*fig. 97*). Here Rousseau is entirely himself. The forest has become a tropical jungle. This time the figure wears a turn-of-the-century dress and hat. Her feet hidden by the grass, and an open umbrella placed horizontally over her shoulder, she is shown walking in an unreal space, wholly delimited by the artist's imagination.

These three paintings provide us with touchstones for understanding Rousseau's art. We have seen how to account for the mastery of the earliest of his surviving landscapes: by a lucky coincidence he was able to rise above the beginner's level. Some later paintings will appear as though they must have been executed earlier, because they are clumsier, but this is not so. It is simply that in them he addressed himself to problems which did not arise in *Carnival Evening*. All that is puzzling is our expectation of a more normal development, one where traditional problems are met and solved one by one, in the traditional academic order. Rousseau excels in those elements of painting which belong to the domain of sensibility, which cannot be learned. On the other hand, he is laborious whenever he tries to perfect those routine elements which pertain to the means of expression. He juggles forms, trying to fit them into his vision. Several small landscapes represent Rousseau's earliest attempts in this direction and give evidence of his apprenticeship as a painter (*figs. 29–33*).

Strange as it may seem, Rousseau's starting point was direct observation: visual stimulation. Two drawings of 1885 show this (*figs. 27 and 28*). His hand is patiently seeking equivalents for what his eye perceives. The lines are redrawn insistently in the effort to record reality. Rousseau was trying to set down his

Luxembourg Gardens, Chopin Monument, 1909

direct experience. But what happened? Some parts of the composition—the fence, for instance—are treated in accordance with the conventional logic of perspective, but they suddenly go astray and become unbalanced, as though moved by the impact of an irrational force. At once a note of awkwardness makes itself felt, although this sudden irrational vibration is nothing but a sign of Rousseau's dissatisfaction. His sensibility ceases to be in tune with his expression. Was not a dissatisfaction of the same kind—though consciously recognized as such—at the root of Cubism? Rousseau did his best to cope with it. His senses demanded something different from what he was capable of achieving with the traditional means of expression, but he was far, very far, from realizing this; hence the state of perpetual compromise which characterizes his painting. I can see no other explanation for his persistent clumsiness: it bespeaks Rousseau's inability to assimilate certain rules which his sensibility rejects. Why must a square window have a trapezoidal shape when seen in perspective? This, in a nutshell, was what bothered Rousseau. Had his sensibility been less intense, he could have adjusted easily, following the rule of reason, and learned the pictorial conventions: his hand was gifted enough. In other words, what we call clumsiness here is a form of Rousseau's originality, although it was unconscious on his part—and something he tried to run away from. Rousseau was the very opposite of the modern artist who says, "This form is thus-and-so because I feel it this way." On the contrary, his first personal experiments were extremely timid. All the early small landscapes are set against vast horizons; views from a distance, they thereby obviate difficulties of construction, making differentiations unnecessary. Conceived somewhat as miniatures are—with a single, clearly defined, compact frontal plane—these landscapes reflect Rousseau's timidity even in their treatment. Very thin brush strokes trace leaves and blades of grass, rendered in almost imperceptibly nuanced colors. To achieve an effect of depth or distance, which helps to focus the vision, Rousseau most often keeps a horizontal area in the foreground (*fig. 29*). In relation to it he sets up his verticals—the trees or, as a variation, factory chimneys (these last may occur anywhere in his landscapes). Thus, step by step, he invariably ends by organizing the whole around a visual center which plays the part of a vanishing point, but which is not one, strictly speaking. Hence the strange effect of relief in Rousseau's paintings, which is increasingly asserted as his hand becomes bolder. In the last analysis, this effect of relief is produced by his colors, interpreted by his forms.

It is time to speak of Rousseau's color. Here his instinct is infallible. Thanks to records kept by Lefevre-Foinet, we know the composition of Rousseau's palette, and its simplicity surprises us. Few painters have achieved such rich nuances with so few colors. One painter has counted more than fifty different shades of green in *The Dream (colorplate, page 133)*. It was no accident that Rousseau painted so many flower pieces. For him they were almost a form of relaxation, and they reflect his pictorial instinct at its purest. Their realization involved no problems, and if their quality is uneven—if they occasionally lack the deep concentration disclosed by Rousseau's most successful creations—it is because he executed them with such facility. He could paint flowers almost mechanically, chiefly because he did not hesitate to paint the same flower piece over and over again. However, most of these that have come down to us date from the last years of his life. I mention them here because they provide a striking example of the power of Rousseau's color *(colorplate, page 121)*.

From the first of Rousseau's works to the last, not one can be named that has been spoiled by his handling of color. On the contrary, the quickest way to recognize a counterfeit Rousseau (and unfortunately there are many) is to study the colors. Although Rousseau's forms can be imitated with relative ease, his color sense is inimitable. It is to color that Rousseau's paintings owe their tightly knit organization and their compact luminosity; in a fake Rousseau, the color is imprecise, dull, and—if the imitation is a bold one—the colors display a rigidity which, instead of linking the forms, divorces them from one another. By contrast, Rousseau's colors, always distinct and strong, never clash. That is his great secret.

Needless to say, Rousseau's color develops over the years, but its development is anything but parallel with that of his art as a whole. It is always far ahead of the forms; the pace is different, for the painter displays much greater confidence in his use of color. At a very early date Rousseau's color achieves a freedom which his forms will never equal. The tiny brush strokes of the early landscapes soon give way to more ample ones. Inconspicuous, almost concealed, and astonishingly light, they sustain the forms like a kind of internal breathing. Consider Rousseau's finest early work, *L'Octroi (colorplate, page 37)*, which in my opinion dates from before 1890. From that year forward, as we shall see, problems of a different order predominate in his paintings.

In the very earliest landscapes, as in all his works, Rousseau starts with a dominant color—green in *L'Octroi*. A photograph of the site *(fig. 19)*, which the painting follows closely, shows the artist's creative approach. The cityscape has been transformed into a rural scene. A plot of grass has replaced the pavement. The whole picture is built on greens. When we examine the nuances, the transitions in the foliage from darker to lighter greens, ending in the yellow at the edge of the foliage, or when we notice the right half of the plot of grass, which is of a much bluer green than the other half, or again when we see the tiny, dark blue cart up against the black railings, we cannot but feel how the presence of air between things blurs the colors and must conclude that Rousseau was trying to express aerial perspective. He has noticed the effects of distance on colors and tries to express it. This is a surprising discovery on the part of a painter as resistant to linear perspective as Rousseau, for aerial perspective is no more than a complement or refinement of the latter. Better than anything else, it may account for one of Rousseau's peculiarities, namely, that his sensitivity to color, his highly developed pictorial sense, actually impaired his plastic sense. This seems probable to me, considering that experience of color is direct and immediate, whereas that of form and three-dimensional space depends upon reflection.   119

The composition of *L'Octroi* shows how carefully Rousseau constructed his painting. However, he does not go beyond certain very striking, though superficial, optical effects, such as that of the thin parallel lines of the railing, a movement echoed in graver tones by the row of cypresses and completed by the little window at the center, to which the eye is led by the slanting roads. This is certainly one of Rousseau's most successful compositions; but the conception of color in it is, by comparison, a far greater achievement. The light diffused in the colors, a light which radiates from the forms without precise direction but subtle in its indecisiveness is, I think, what animates the painting and endows it with such extraordinary power.

Thus, the technique of Rousseau's landscapes is characterized from the outset by uncertainty with respect to construction and great subtlety in the handling of color. The forms are altered slowly or remain almost unchanged, whereas the brush stroke acquires increasing ease at an early date. It becomes an articulate means, manipulated with great sureness, as we recognize at once in the way Rousseau paints trees. This is the key element in his art, the most faithful mirror of his sensibility. Rousseau's old familiarity with foliage makes him apply each discovery to it before applying it to anything else. Foliage serves as the locus of the first battles he fought and won. In it we can best follow the evolution of his brush stroke, an evolution that became more rapid once he became aware of aerial perspective and learned to render it. Rousseau, who never learned to place an object in space, paints the most beautiful trees there are, though his competence falters when he starts on the tree trunks. This profound experience of foliage, of its tremulous mode of being in space, blazes the trail for him, after which the other elements of his art follow at a considerable distance. Consider, for instance, the painting entitled *The Painter and His Model (fig. 74).* We can hardly believe that the hand which executed such trees also executed these human figures. They are as clumsy as the foliage is refined—indeed so refined as almost to have become routine. This confirms our view that the development of Rousseau's brush stroke was rapid only in the treatment of vegetation. Certain forms lag behind others—as though the painter had executed them at a different age—and this will persist to the end. If in a painting such as *The Painter and His Model* the forms of the trees seem to be the work of a more mature artist than the one who painted the human figures —though clearly both are part of the same work—the difference is even more marked when we compare successive paintings. This is why all of Rousseau's early portraits, though strictly contemporaneous with the landscapes, seem to have been painted before the latter. Our eye finds it difficult to assimilate such a close juxtaposition of clumsiness and skill; our mind hesitates to ascribe them to one and the same period. And yet this is the case with Rousseau's painting.

Although Rousseau's landscapes can be situated chronologically—for instance, we know that *Carnival Evening* is one of his earliest works—we have no precise points of reference in the case of the portraits. Moreover, since the evolution of his art varies from one genre to another, our knowledge of his de-

Vase of Flowers (second version), 1909

velopment in landscape is no help in determining the development of his portrait painting. At best it can serve as an auxiliary postulate, confirming where necessary that Rousseau's art does indeed change with time, however irregularly and puzzlingly at first sight. Rousseau's development follows a line all its own; it is up to us to reconstruct it.

In keeping with our method, we shall begin our investigations with the first portrait which can be dated with absolute certainty. This is the self-portrait entitled *Portrait-Landscape*, which was exhibited in 1890 *(colorplate, page 31)*. Biographical data has enabled us to identify some retouches, such as the name of Joséphine, and some additions, like the academic insignia. These alterations merely have psychological significance, but they will be useful when we try to establish the chronological order of Rousseau's portraits.

A whole series of portraits is infinitely more ponderous in comparison with *Portrait-Landscape*, which is characterized by a free, sweeping technique, revealing that they must have preceded it. This appears especially certain in the case of the two oval portraits *(figs. 25 and 26)*, which are incontestably those of Rousseau and his first wife. We recognize the painter by his little beard and his wife by the expression of the mouth—an expression which recurs in her face shown floating in the sky in the painting entitled *Present and Past (fig. 43)*. The rudimentary aspect of these two portraits, their dimensions—they are hardly larger than postcards—certainly suggest the beginner. What is striking are the colors—black and white; what holds our attention is the woman's expression—the unusual lines that form her eyes.

The clumsiness peculiar to these two portraits, seeming to derive from some as yet unleashed inner power, is also found in a group portrait *(fig. 42)* which has been connected with the painting *Baby's Party*, exhibited in 1903. The affinities between this group portrait and the two little portraits are obvious. The thickly applied color suggests that Rousseau had a great deal of trouble executing it. This was no doubt one of his first attempts at a composition involving several human figures. His brush stubbornly goes back again and again over the same areas and is only at ease with the foliage, which, clearly, does not interest the painter here. Curiously, this painting goes to two extremes: Rousseau's hand displays the maximum diligence in treatment of the figures, which are all but squashed by the thickness of the paint, whereas the foliage is painted almost mechanically. Since we know that artists are particularly attached to works on which they have spent a great deal of effort, I am inclined to believe that this group portrait is the painting that was exhibited in 1891 under the title *The M. Family*, but it must have been painted before *Portrait-Landscape* and before *Past and Present*.

I do not hesitate to situate *Past and Present* among Rousseau's earliest works, contrary to various hypotheses advanced concerning it. Because of the caption which originally accompanied it ("Being separated from each other / From those they had loved / Both enter a new union / Remaining faithful to their thoughts"), it was identified as the painting exhibited in 1907 under the title *Philosophical Thought*. This identification may be correct; in the catalogue of the Indépendants it was described as "owned by M. R." The initials certainly stood for "Monsieur Rousseau," and it is very possible that he sent this painting to the Salon since it represented his two dead wives and thus would have had special significance for him. However, the work could not have been painted as late as 1907. Moreover, the date inscribed next to the signature is hard to decipher and has been misread. This is why the painting has until now been mistaken for a late work. It has been interpreted as a sort of regression in the artist's development and has long been dated after 1900 on the grounds that it shows Rousseau's second wife, and that he is himself pictured in it without a beard.

Nonetheless, it seems to us more natural to link this work with the group portrait of *The M. Family*, if only because of the similarity between the ivy plant in the former and the trailing branches in the latter work. Closer inspection reveals that the vegetation is painted in Rousseau's early manner, which is very different from his later style. And then there is another important detail: the two heads, that of Rousseau's second wife and his own, have been repainted. We can see clearly how he painted out some of his own hair—there is a dark area around the head—and also some of the hair of the female figure. The latter head, needless to say, has been entirely redone. Rousseau also painted out the beard he had worn as a young man. It was perhaps at the time he reworked the picture that he had the strange idea of painting in the sky the two earlier heads he had obliterated. In short, what we have is an early work partly repainted after 1900. What was done here is not so different from what was done in the instance of *Portrait-Landscape*: subsequent developments in the painter's life were added one by one over the years. Rousseau's candor is touching: it just occurs to me that the few white hairs in the beard in *Portrait-Landscape* may have been the very last of the added touches!

Clearly, Rousseau was in the habit of partly revising his works, sometimes many years later. This has created further difficulties in the task of dating them, but at the same time awareness of this habit helps us solve the riddle of a painting such as the *Portrait of Pierre Loti (fig. 48)*. It is most often dated 1910 on the basis of its over-all plastic effect, but the moment we scrutinize it more carefully, we are obliged to recognize obvious retouches. We notice that the foliage, both at the top and at the right, ends abruptly along a slightly indented line parallel to the edge of the canvas. Clearly, when painting the foliage, the artist ran into some sort of obstacle—and this could only have been the edge of a frame. In other words, the foliage, which is in Rousseau's later manner, was added after the work had been framed. Moreover, the narrow marginal strip which the brush could not then reach still shows the green of the former foliage. I believe the face was painted over also, because it discloses analogies with Rousseau's last portraits. There is only the one telltale strip—the rest of the picture was left as it had been painted earlier. In the light of the iconographic details mentioned before (see page 46), we must conclude that

24 *Notre-Dame from Quai Henri IV* (study for *Notre-Dame*), 1909

Notre-Dame, 1909

this portrait was painted in 1891–92, at a moment when Pierre Loti was very much in the news. Laboratory tests would be required to establish the exact extent of the repainting, but in any event we know enough to exempt this work from the ordinary chronological sequence in attempting to retrace the artist's development (see note 1, page 310).

In this connection, the portrait entitled *Portrait of a Young Girl (fig. 45)* may serve as a more reliable touchstone. Formally speaking, it marks a stage of development beyond *Present and Past*, and at the same time prefigures the large portraits Rousseau painted about 1895 when his technique underwent a change. The slow, ponderous treatment of every detail in this painting reminds us of the early works, whereas the over-all conception as expressed in the frontality of the figure foreshadows the subsequent portraits. In his stubborn effort to solve a problem he has not encountered before, Rousseau stresses the foreground in the closely spaced row of tree trunks, which push the figure forward and at the same time emphasize its verticality. The resulting contrast endows the portrait with the monumental character which we will find more fully developed in later portraits, and which bespeaks a highly personal vision (see note 2, page 310).

This brings us to Rousseau's *Portrait-Landscape*, one of his major works. It combines all his previous discoveries and foreshadows what is to come. We have seen that the World's Fair of 1889 marked a turning point in his life and influenced his art in various ways. *Portrait-Landscape* reflects a new ease in his manipulation of the means of expression: the forms have become smaller and more compact. In this work everything in the left side of the picture—the bridge, the flag-bedecked ship, the water, the trees, the houses, the Eiffel Tower—marks a daring advance for Rousseau.

What we have here is a figuration of space according to the immediate perceptions of the sensibility; and especially remarkable is the fact that it is realized in purely descriptive terms. Here, the experienced painter stands aside to give expression to the naïve man that he really was. He has even ventured to put a balloon in the sky—to be sure, motivated by the desire to tell a story, but also as a sign of new-found expressive freedom. There is the same pictorial daring in his placement of the dark, flat area of the human figure in empty space.

Second Period: After 1890

It is in his treatment of flat areas that we detect the change that has taken place in Rousseau's art. This change will become more and more explicit in the years to come. It was from about 1890 on that Rousseau looked about him for assistance in solving technical problems and found it in the study of academic painters—for example, in the technique of a painting like *The Centenary of Independence (colorplate, page 45)*, which dates from 1892 and employs glazes in the construction of the forms, just as the best academic practice recommends. Their tradition of art was in its death throes, but Rousseau saw them as the leading contemporary painters. Being a self-taught artist, Rousseau could not possibly identify himself with the Impressionists, who at this time were treated as outcasts no less than he was himself. In looking for guidance, he could only address himself to the illustrious teachers at the Ecole des Beaux-Arts. That he should have done so is surely the most logical and easily explained step in his artistic development. Although he had applied to the Louvre for a copyist's card as early as 1884, the immense museum must have bewildered him. He was not cultivated enough to find his way around in the painting of the past. He went straight to that of the present, which he saw at the Salon des Artistes Français— the salon of Bouguereau. It is possible that the great exhibition of French painting, which was one of the attractions of the 1889 World's Fair, also influenced him. However that may be, it is obvious that from 1890 on Rousseau had been studying academic works. Moreover, it is only natural that he needed several years of painting experience before his eye was sufficiently trained to derive technical profit from the study of other works.

Until now, Rousseau as painter had merely been doing "what comes naturally." Most of his drawings must date from the early years, and if only we possessed those 200 drawings he referred to in 1895, we would be able to trace his development in detail. For we would see how he worked when simply confronting nature, without recourse to models, and we would have a record of progress of his capacity for observation. We would be able to see what most appealed to him and to trace his growing competence with the pencil. In short, we would have a more spontaneous image of the artist's personality than his paintings give us, alternating as they do between spontaneity and repression.

Among the few extant drawings by Rousseau, two seem to belong to the first period. One of them *(fig. 44)* shows a seated girl whose skirt is not unlike that of *Portrait of a Young Girl*, whereas her formless hands recall the figures in Rousseau's earliest paintings. In addition to these elements which place the drawing in the period before 1890, we find a third one: the girl is shown eating. At the bottom right we see a bottle and a glass, oddly tilted. The drawing has come down to us in poor condition, damaged by dampness, but I think I can guess at the action thanks to the head of a dog at the bottom. The dog has knocked over the bottle and the glass and Rousseau has tried to portray them as they are beginning to fall. Could this be a preliminary sketch for a lost painting entitled *Le dîner sur l'herbe*, which was exhibited in 1888? This is probable. If so, the second drawing *(fig. 53)* would be of about the same date: it is characterized by the same analytical movement of line, the same attentive vision which this time seeks to define what is seen in successive planes.

These two drawings seem to confirm Rousseau's statement that his first teacher was nature. The hatchings in the drawing are replaced with brushwork in the painting. His brush strokes are timid and tiny at first, but they gradually take on strength: this is Rousseau's first style, developed with the help of drawing—that is to say, through direct observation. But although the early brush stroke can effectively reproduce the vegetal world from which it derives, it cannot transpose forms. An essential problem arises in Rousseau's early painting, which might be formulated as follows: how is it possible, in terms of an imperfect technique, to construct a homogeneous, smooth surface such as a human figure? We recognize here the pictorial counterpart of the major plastic problem of perspective. It may well have been the tremendous difficulties Rousseau ran into with the human figure that induced him to turn for guidance to academic painting. This occurred around 1890.

Recognizing that the oil medium was unsatisfactory when it came to rendering the cross-hatching of drawing, Rousseau tried to discover the secret of the academic painters whose finished forms, once the pictures have been varnished, show nothing of the brushwork. This is evidenced by the change in his technique after 1890. It was at this time that Rousseau began to "study". He himself gives us the names of his teachers: Clément, Gérôme, Bonnat. He cites these names over and over again. Our research has included examination of their works and casts light on Rousseau's odd apprenticeship to them. Rousseau probably actually met Clément when he began to paint, but the other two impressed him more. And it is interesting to see how in the end he did profit from the study of forms diametrically opposed to his own temperament. Of course, the word "study" is a highly inexact term for what Rousseau did. Once again, we must be wary of bringing our conventional standards to bear. This was a sort of influence which does not involve any real affinity, for the lesson learned was turned to most unacademic ends, refracted as it was through Rousseau's unique vision. He was a prism through which the most threadbare, banal elements of academic painting were broken down and reconstituted with new power and relevance. It seems incredible, but Rousseau really learned something from Bonnat's solemn blacks and whites. Rousseau had always been attracted to these extremes of color, most often keeping them for his portraits, no doubt because he felt them to be impressive. But how differently he used black and white after 1890! The finest example is *Child on the Rocks (colorplate, page 59)*, a work Rousseau was commissioned to paint in commemoration of a child that died. Rousseau's extraordinary feeling for the gravity of black—we are told that Gauguin admired Rousseau's blacks—here reaches its highest pitch.

Think of a typical Bonnat—the *Portrait of Madame Pasca*, for instance, with its ample black cape trimmed with a thin strip of white fur. Concerned merely with imitating what he actually sees, Rousseau does not imitate the Bonnat but is inspired by it to completely original expression. Rousseau doubtless supposed he was imitating it, perhaps even that he was copying, but actually he broadened the scope of his own powers. His contact with academic works deepened his own plastic resources, and in this connection Gérôme was even more useful to him than Bonnat.

Gérôme, who was Manet's great adversary, was Rousseau's teacher par excellence. Here again it is a case of influence without affinity, but beside technique Rousseau drew upon Gérôme's subject matter. Everything about Gérôme's painting attracted Rousseau. I am almost tempted to think that he turned to other "teachers" for his portraits only because Gérôme painted very few portraits. Rousseau's interest in Gérôme must have lasted a long time. Two of Rousseau's works, *The Sleeping Gypsy (colorplate, page 65)* and *Happy Quartet (fig. 76)*, executed five years apart, unmistakably recall paintings by Gérôme, as we shall see later. In the light of this we cannot help thinking that if today most of Gérôme's works were not so scattered as to be inaccessible, study of them would disclose other points of contact with Rousseau's painting. It is enough to mention that Gérôme repeatedly painted wild animals: *Lioness Meeting a Jaguar, Love in the Cage of Wild Beasts, St. Jérôme Asleep on His Lion*, for example. But, to repeat, the influence of Gérôme's repertory of forms on Rousseau has yet to be explored more fully.

There can be no doubt that Gérôme's technique greatly influenced Rousseau. Some of the academic painter's forms, which are all very much of a piece, looking as if they had been cut out, were incontestably admired by Rousseau as perfect examples of forceful expression. He did not feel their coldness and conventionality, nor a certain characteristic stiffness, which may be accounted for by the fact that Gérôme was a sculptor as well as a painter. Details from Gérôme's once-famous painting, *Cockfight (fig. 93)*, may well have appealed to Rousseau—for example, the southern vegetation standing out singly and brilliantly against the bright sky or the interlaced pattern of greens. These elements of the work are clearly reminiscent of Rousseau's exotic motifs. Strange as it may seem, Rousseau's development was influenced by Gérôme!

Rousseau's general aesthetic direction, as we have been reconstructing it, helps us to understand the far-reaching changes in his technique which occurred after 1890. We are almost tempted to speak of a second style. From that year on, parallel to but distinct from the earlier technique, which is characterized by small, broken brush strokes, there appears another technique, consisting of sweeping strokes that form flat areas; in Rousseau's eyes this second technique was equivalent to academic relief, though actually it only marked the point beyond which he could not go due to his limited knowledge of the craft. To the end of his life he used one or the other of these two techniques, according to the requirements of the subject, and sometimes he combined them. Both techniques—the broad, flat brush strokes and the hatched brush strokes—will continue to develop.

Rousseau's second technique makes its appearance abruptly with *Storm in the Forest (colorplate, page 41)*, dated 1891, which, in my opinion, was the painting exhibited at the Salon des Indépendants in 1891 under the title *Surprised!* A canvas of these dimensions—51 × 63″—so ambitious in every other respect as well, could have been painted only with a view to exhibiting it in the Salon. The picture, which shows a wild beast about to leap (suggesting the idea of surprise), headed the list of his exhibits that year. This work foreshadows Rousseau's exotic subjects, which do not appear in his painting until 1904, but from then on hold a special, almost indefinable place in his art. In addition to elements that appear here for the first time and that will persist in his works—the flat areas, the brilliant colors—there are others, especially a dynamic tension, which will never recur later. This tension is at bottom alien to Rousseau's temperament. Like the sources of his other famous paintings, the source of this one will undoubtedly one day be discovered, but in the light of the foregoing we are able even now to make some conjectures. Clearly, Rousseau is following a model here—the presence of a tension alien to his nature proves it. I believe that his choice of subject comprised two stages. First, he had the idea of painting a wild animal, an idea no doubt inspired by Gérôme's paintings. This would have dignified the subject in Rousseau's eyes. Then came a second stage when Rousseau decided to paint the animal about to spring, following his given model, and giving free rein to his imagination only in the treatment of details. Rousseau's model for this painting (in which vegetation for the first time in his work takes on aspects of unreality) was probably an illustration in a children's book. We know for a fact that Rousseau was inspired by such books.

At this time, moreover, Rousseau had many other sources of inspiration. We have seen that a number of his paintings such as *Storm at Sea (fig. 54)*, *The Centenary of Independence (colorplate, page 45)*, and *View of the Pont de Grenelle (fig. 57)* were inspired by the 1889 World's Fair.

Like *Storm in the Forest*, the subject of *Storm at Sea*, a transatlantic liner tossed about by waves, stands alone in Rousseau's work. But here the expression of movement is congenial to the painter's temperament, and his technique is characterized by an intimacy and immediacy which mark the more personal pole of his art.

By contrast, *The Centenary of Independence* and the second version of it which is entitled *The Carmagnole (fig. 55)* are evidence of Rousseau's maturity. In his own way he now dominates all his problems. He is familiar with his means of expression and handles them with facility. It is enough to note how he transposes the subject of *The Centenary of Independence* into the horizontal format of *The Carmagnole*, and how he rearranges the same forms in the new space. There is real assurance in his use of color, in his subtle nuances of light—

The Muse Inspiring the Poet (first version), 1909

blues over ocher, ochers over brown. Now that he has surmounted a number of technical difficulties, Rousseau is able to tell a story with full freedom, and to weave an atmosphere around it. The dancers convey the public euphoria of a holiday celebration, and this ability to evoke a content over and beyond the immediate subject is a sign of maturity.

It is interesting to note that now the contradictory elements in Rousseau's style do not clash, but combine to form a coherent whole. For instance, his vision is simultaneously synthetic and analytic: the tiniest leaf may show the structure of a form seen close up, while a human figure next to it, for all its larger size, is painted like a distant area, without details. Distance does not determine the aspect of things, nor does plausibility: next to some highly descriptive form may appear a form whose function is purely aesthetic—without logical foundation and yet, by its presence, strengthening the over-all effect of reality. This, for instance, is evident in the case of the white bush or tree at the extreme left of *The Centenary of Independence*. Rousseau also displays new freedom in his treatment of perspective, introducing several points of view. Quite inadvertently, once again, he touches upon the problem of Cubism and solves it with the most naïve inconsistency. Whereas the big central tree is painted as if it were the axis of the vanishing point, toward which flagpoles and banners converge, a second opening into space is created by the arrangement of the colors, so that the eye is led almost diagonally through the painting—from the aristocrats in the foreground at the right, via the circle of dancers, to the children in the background at the left. What an enrichment of pictorial space!

Rousseau is now a veteran painter; he can permit himself every liberty. His style maintains a perfect balance. His mastery is strikingly illustrated in the composition of *View of the Pont de Grenelle (fig. 57)*, where a horizontal format complicates the painter's task. In the case of *The Carmagnole*, which has the same format, the task was partly facilitated by the circumstance that Rousseau had merely to transpose a previously treated subject. In *View of the Pont de Grenelle*, however, the problem was entirely new, and the marvelously flexible horizontality of this snowy landscape would alone be sufficient to refute the opinion frequently advanced that Rousseau was a primitive painter. He was a primitive only in the sense that no barrier of culture stood between him and his art; he was not a primitive in the sense of being a clumsy painter. Rousseau's clumsiness must not be confused with incompetence. It reflects his need to raise forms to the level of perception, and his distortions are timid versions of the deliberate distortions to be found in much modern painting, including Picasso's. With Rousseau, clumsiness attains the rank of a style. It is the indispensable foundation for understanding his painting, and it is the more difficult to grasp because the inferiority complex of the self-taught artist is bound up with it. But it is easy to distinguish between the tenseness of a brush stroke intimidated by a subject and the brush stroke that expresses the painter's personal feeling in form. Thus, there can be no question of some innate clumsiness which persists throughout Rousseau's career as a painter. Once he got beyond his apprentice

The Dream, 1910

phase, there was no longer any incompetence in his painting. This is confirmed by the hushed atmosphere that characterizes *View of the Pont de Grenelle*. Now, Rousseau knows how to rise above the subject to pictorial content.

This transformation, which is the supreme goal of painting, takes place with even greater intensity in the famous painting *War (colorplate, page 55)*, which Rousseau exhibited in 1894. It is looked upon as an altogether exceptional work, which in every respect stands out from the others, but in reality it represents the consummate realization of the mature Rousseau's powers.

Rousseau's Creative Imagination: *War, The Sleeping Gypsy*

In *War* Rousseau's creative imagination takes wing, and no hesitation checks its course. A single breath animates this canvas, which seems to have been executed at a single stroke. Rousseau's biography supplies the psychological explanation for his self-confidence: it was the effect of Jarry's friendship.

On the purely aesthetic plane, the lithograph published in *L'Imagier* takes on special importance, because when we compare it with the painting, we are able for the first time to trace Rousseau's progress from the sketch to the oil version of a work. Since, moreover, we happen to have clues as to Rousseau's choice of subject, this is the one work by him which lets us follow the course of its creation. Here, if nowhere else, we can treat Rousseau like any other artist, without being plagued by gaps in our knowledge.

We know that *War* was inspired by Georgin's *The Battle of the Pyramids (fig. 20, page 52)*. What does Rousseau take from the latter? The answer is easy: he takes the idea of the foreground, the arrangement of bodies fallen on the battlefield. We even understand why, for invariably it is the foreground that gives Rousseau the greatest trouble in composition. Most often he solves the problem by leaving the foreground empty, so that the eye is led directly into depth. Georgin's solution to the problem obviously impressed him; he follows it in the lithograph and at the same time carries it further. This is the only instance we know of Rousseau being inspired by Georgin; the other details that relate the lithograph to the popular print were part of the prevailing image of war—the galloping horse, for instance, and the brandished sword. But Rousseau's breadth of vision manifests itself at once. The galloping warrior as a symbol of war is changed to a formless creature with a woman's face. Furthermore, the idea of devastation is added to that of struggle: fire follows in the wake of the sword, and the trees have already been shattered. These departures from the model show how different Rousseau's art is from the popular prints to which it is sometimes likened. Whereas it is true that Rousseau expresses the spirit of the common people, it is completely erroneous to suppose that he was attracted by folk art as such. Not he, but Jarry, the intellectual, was fond of the *Épinal* prints; it was Rémy de Gourmont, the belated romantic and former student at the Ecole des Chartes, who sensed their value; Rousseau, we have seen, loved Gérôme and Bouguereau. Even though he introduces the freshness of folk art into painting, he turns his back on folk art as such. This is clear from his casual exposure to Georgin—an exposure brought about by Jarry in the first place. Neither the rigidity of forms in the popular color print nor their regular repetition of motives influences him. If he borrows a subject from them here, he proceeds immediately to broaden it and make it more abstract, thereby going counter to the very spirit of the popular print. Only once during his entire career did Rousseau come close to the style. This was in 1906, in the painting *Liberty Inviting the Artists . . . (colorplate, page 89).* Here he was no doubt carried away by the solemn character of the subject, though this applies chiefly to the accessory figure of the angel. The very fact that Rousseau could come to be considered an artist in this period points to the extinction of folk art. It seems natural to me that his own ambitions, whatever their realization, went in the opposite direction—that is, in the direction of academic painting. Such reflections follow from the comparison of Rousseau's lithograph with popular prints.

The elaboration of the subject undertaken by Rousseau lets us glimpse his manner of thought and helps us grasp the creative process involved in the transition from lithograph to final oil version. In the latter Rousseau keeps the same elements, but he clarifies them, orders them, and endows them with strength. For this purpose he resorts to an entirely different scheme of composition. Whereas in the lithograph the forms all converge upon the horse, in the painting he goes back to a pattern reminiscent of *The Centenary of Independence.* Between the two large trees he sets up an optical diagonal which is stressed by the white sword, but at the same time by showing the horse frontally he restores a central vanishing point. The multiple viewpoint is at the service of the subject; unbalanced, the scene departs from familiar reality, thereby drawing the viewer into an extreme situation. Almost none of Rousseau's paintings reach out to capture the viewer's attention to this extent. The painter has gone much farther than the draftsman. *War* makes us realize to what extent Rousseau constructs with color, to what extent he thinks in color. The steel grays, blues, and phosphorescent reds are so conceived as to reinforce one another. Usually content to be an observer, Rousseau here plunges headlong into the visionary, and what strikes us most is the ampleness of his imagination. To the sense of the horrible, which he arouses with the rotting corpses, he adds a feeling of revulsion by piling up jagged, trailing forms: the monstrously long mane of the horse, the animal-like hair of the galloping figure, and its torn white garment, which by contrast strengthens the effect of the blacks. Rousseau's imagination makes our revulsion complete by conveying terror: it is a nightmarish picture.

At this point we realize that, even though we may be able to come closer to Rousseau's art by investigating his specific idiom and thereby gaining an approximate idea of his creative approach, his imagination will forever elude us. Like some suddenly, dramatically opened fissure, *War* affords us a glimpse into the artist's imagination, after which his work closes up again on this extreme range of his sensibility. We should never have suspected its existence from what went before, nor will we be given another glimpse of it later on. Baffling in itself, *War* is even more baffling in the context of Rousseau's other works.

The picture is a solitary monument to buried depths in the artist, compared to which his habitual vision is an untroubled, unchanging surface. Rousseau himself must have been as baffled by it as we are ourselves. By accident he gave free rein to his imagination just this once, but he could not possibly cultivate it, distrusting all his powers of invention as he did, and preferring to follow a model. Rousseau was quick to repress that part of himself which came to the surface in *War*.

With this in mind, we may approach *The Sleeping Gypsy* (*colorplate, page 65*), exhibited in 1897, three years after *War*. It is a very different picture—indeed, it is the result of everything Rousseau repressed. *War* was an incursion into the realm of the fantastic (and Jarry may have played a large part in this), whereas *The Sleeping Gypsy*, which Rousseau intended as a realistic painting, is not at all realistic, since its unusual formal character is under the sway of the artist's repressed imagination. A painting by Gérôme, *The Two Majesties* (*fig. 22, page 64*), served as the model for Rousseau's famous work, though the latter added a few commonplace features (*see page 66*). The forms are determined by Rousseau's technical competence, which was considerable at the time. All in all, the finished painting achieves a depth of originality which leaves us perplexed. We cannot help recalling the ghost story Rousseau used to invoke to explain the formal features of his painting: he maintained that his dead wife guided his hand. For all its crudity, does not this story suggest the feelings of a man whose powers of creation extend beyond his own powers of understanding?

The Sleeping Gypsy expresses the very fact that the artist's intentions have been left far behind by the work. Rousseau was very explicit about what he intended to represent in this painting: "A wandering Negress, playing the mandolin, with her jar next to her." With literal simplicity, he adds that her jar is "a vessel containing drinking water." But his imagination overruled the scrupulous literalness of his approach, transforming the work in a way the painter could not anticipate. No painting in the history of art is more flagrantly at odds with the painter's intention in painting it. This is a striking example of the magic of Rousseau's art, unmistakable in this indefinable painting, but always

Study for *View of Parc Montsouris*, about 1910

operative to some extent in all his pictures. Rousseau's ambiguous status as an artist was what provoked it. No sooner had he drawn a form, than it was amplified by the subliminal force of his imagination, which he kept so firmly in control (or so he thought). This is how reality comes to take on such strange relief in his art. We think of it as an element of Rousseau's originality, whereas he did all he could to stifle all evidence of his reactions to things. He repressed sensation in the name of pictorial convention, and in revenge sensation gave rise to unexpected forms—tiny figures who turn their backs on the viewer, opening doors leading nowhere, and trees that surge upward to anywhere at all. This movement of conflicting forces ultimately endows Rousseau's realism with a hallucinatory character, especially pronounced in such paintings as *L'Octroi (colorplate, page 37)* and *Fishermen (fig. 149)*.

His determination to repress his imagination is part of Rousseau's creative process. Not until the very end of his life did he allow it to appear in his painting, but even then he tried to tame it, confining it to a restricted sphere— tropical landscapes. This is the only area in which Rousseau's creative imagination and pictorial instinct became one, unhampered by consciousness.

Before addressing ourselves to Rousseau's last works, we must briefly characterize his painting in the period we have been discussing, the period of which *War* and *The Sleeping Gypsy* are the high points. The titles of works exhibited at the Salon des Indépendants, as well as the gradual development of his idiom, will guide us. Unfortunately, however, there is no perfect correspondence between the list of titles and the works that survive. Only through formal analysis can we deduce that *Portrait of a Woman (fig. 70)* was painted before another, large portrait of a woman *(fig. 69)*. It is generally thought that the latter portrait represents Rousseau's first wife and that it was painted in 1890. Although we cannot determine with absolute certainty the identity of the person portrayed, aesthetic evidence places the portrait much later than 1890. The forms are far more flexible and much less timid and rigid than in the *Portrait-Landscape* of 1890; moreover, it discloses that Rousseau was beginning to loosen up his forms. Consequently, we must assume that some years went by before his new flexible manner asserted itself. For my part, I place these two portraits around 1895. The first *(fig. 69)* may have been exhibited as early as 1892, and the second *(fig. 70)* after 1895, perhaps as late as 1897. Their dimensions (one is 50″ high, the other 78³/₄″) make it certain that they were both exhibited at the Salon des Indépendants.

We cannot say even this much concerning the landscapes that constituted the greater part of Rousseau's output in these years. Most of them seem to belong to the large number of works that never went to the Salon. Which ones did he exhibit? It is impossible to know this since in many instances these landscapes are not dated and the subjects were treated again later. Nor does topographic evidence help, for the sites in question have changed beyond recognition. All we can do is conjecture about a chronological order based on the comparative degree of plastic freedom the pictures disclose.

Closer analysis of the painting entitled *Path in Parc Montsouris (fig. 61)*, for which we have an oil study *(fig. 60)*, will help us here. Because of the surprising freedom of the study, it has been supposed that the work was painted late in Rousseau's life, around 1910. But it is enough to compare it with a really late work—entitled *View of Parc Montsouris (fig. 139)*—to realize that it must have been done earlier. The brushwork removes all doubts on this score. More than that, the two excessively large trees reflect Rousseau's effort to emphasize the foreground which, as we have seen, was gradually receiving more careful treatment. On the other hand, when we compare the finished painting with the study and with a late landscape such as *View from the Pont d'Austerlitz (fig. 162)*, which is nearly as free in its brushwork as the study, we grasp another of Rousseau's features: he displays increasing freedom in execution, and the degree to which a given painting is "finished" in relation to the preliminary sketch thus provides a supplementary clue as to date.

For these reasons we shall not hesitate to affirm that the work shown in figure 61 is the painting that was exhibited in the Salon of 1895. Thus, the existence of the preliminary study becomes particularly significant. It shows us not only to what extent Rousseau was an artist, but also that his freedom of technique and of vision, latent in his art, were far from satisfying his conceptions of art. We can also see to what extent his ideas on art were in conflict with his instinct.

The fact that Rousseau was painting oil sketches as early as 1895 suggests that the so-called studies he exhibited in the group show "Chez le Barc de Boutteville" in the fall of 1894 may well have been sketches of this type. The fact that these sketches after nature appear so early—not about 1898, as had been supposed—is a detail that actually ought not to surprise us. It can be accounted for without invoking Rousseau's spontaneously free vision, which at the time could hardly have been suspected from the finished works. Rousseau was always at ease with trees and sky; attracted by what he saw, he was tempted to capture it, to paint it from life, to perform the primordial, "original" act of painting. His hand was competent enough to do so. And in addition to the pleasure of yielding to this temptation, the sketches provided Rousseau with a model to be followed later—and he always felt a great need for models. Thus, almost schizophrenically, he first gratified his painter's instinct, only to subjugate it later to the demands of consciousness. Unable to surmount his contradictions within the actual pictorial space, he surmounted them by indulging heart and head alternately in time. However, by granting even provisional freedom to his instinct, Rousseau inevitably served his apprenticeship to pictorial freedom pure and simple. Inadvertently, Rousseau found in his own painting the elements which determined its evolution and paved the way for his own future development. In my opinion, this is the deeper meaning of Rousseau's numerous oil studies.

But a still more curious phenomenon took place. As Rousseau's paintings became freer, his pace quickened and invention began to flag. He went back to certain sketches for fresh inspiration. This was the case with the *View of the Fortifications (fig. 65)*, exhibited in 1896, in which Rousseau faithfully copied a sketch *(fig. 64)*. Several years later he went back to the same subject *(fig. 66)* probably using the same drawing, adding just a few variations, and completing it with the greatest freedom.

Rousseau seems to have proceeded similarly in the case of the landscape entitled *View of the Chair Factory and the Quai de Seine at Alfortville*. We have a "finished" version which is certainly the painting that was exhibited in 1897 *(fig. 146)*, and a second version executed much later *(fig. 147)*.

In the same connection, to compensate for his slowness of invention, Rousseau did not hesitate to copy almost literally a landscape by a little-known contemporary painter, Camille Bernier. This is *Breton Scene (fig. 112)*, based entirely on Bernier's painting *Farm at Bannalec (fig. 113)*. And he went even further. Since he was getting many commissions in this period (1907–08), he made a second version of his own painting *(fig. 114)*.

Nor do I believe that this was an isolated case in his career. On the contrary, I am sure that with further investigation the origins of many of Rousseau's paintings will come to light—certainly of all those whose subjects depart from his habitual repertoire. Such a work as *Winter Landscape (fig. 125)*, for example, seems to follow closely some forgotten illustration.

Last Period: Tropical Landscapes

Rousseau's painting after 1890 was extraordinarily rich, and led to the flowering of his art. The constant constraint with respect to form, which was actually no more than a quest for balance, makes possible some of his finest landscapes, including *Banks of the Seine (colorplate, page 69)*, *Sawmill near Paris (colorplate, page 49)*, and *The Quarry (colorplate, page 61)*. These most balanced of his works constitute the "classic" phase of his style, in which all his means of expression contribute equally to the felicitous result.

During this period Rousseau enlarged his repertoire with a number of flower pieces. To him this subject was a form of relaxation, he excelled in it, and treated it frequently. The earliest flower piece we know is doubtless the painting entitled *Poet's Flowers (fig. 49)*, which by its open-work construction brings to mind Rousseau's earliest experiments. There follows a curious improvisation which bears the date "August 15, 1892" *(fig. 50)*. Rousseau must have enjoyed tossing it off, but the technique discloses his interest at the time in color applied in flat areas. As for his other flower pieces, they are readily assimilable by his other plastic researches and hence may be situated chronologically. The earliest of these is *Vase of Flowers (fig. 51)*, in which Rousseau chooses rare color combinations and handles them with great subtlety. To the last, a flower piece signified a display of color to him, and his almost crude, instinctive freshness protects him from becoming too precious, a pattern into which so many painters of flowers fall.

Rousseau's art was developing by leaps and bounds when suddenly, for two successive years, he stopped exhibiting at the Salon des Indépendants. We still do not know the reasons for this interruption which, however, marks no break from the plastic point of view. No new elements appear in the paintings that follow, so no change seems to have occurred in the interval.

In 1901 Rousseau's principal exhibit was a painting entitled *Unpleasant Surprise (fig. 72)*, the origins of which remain a mystery. This was the first time Rousseau painted a nude against a narrative or anecdotal background; probably the latter was perfectly simple and logical to him, as was *The Sleeping Gypsy*, but to us it remains inscrutable. The following year, in the painting entitled *Happy Quartet (fig. 76)*, Rousseau once again drew upon academic paintings for a source of inspiration. Nor did he just borrow details: he tried to assimilate the spirit of his model. *Happy Quartet* closely follows Gérôme's *Innocence (fig. 75)*.

Like the academic painters, he sets out to represent an abstract idea, and conceives *Happy Quartet*, which is an allegory of love incorporating the obligatory male and female, a little cupid, and a dog, symbol of faithfulness. However, the fairly elaborate iconography does not dominate the painting. Rather, it is dominated by an atmosphere of happiness, by a warm golden light which the large mass of the trees seems to give off from its shimmering foliage. Once again, Rousseau succeeds not by his conscious effort, but by the unconscious finality of his effortless forms.

An analogous attempt, in my opinion, is the *Baby's Party (colorplate, page 73)*, which I would date around this same time. It goes far beyond the model to become a brilliant image of childhood. This painting may very well be the one exhibited at the Salon of 1903. Had it been done later, Rousseau would have treated the face with the analytical insistence of his subsequent portraits. Prior to 1903 he was not able to render that golden light which seems to come from nowhere and yet to be everywhere in the painting.

Similarly, the deliberately luminous colors and the subject induce us to situate the painting *The Tiger Hunt (fig. 135)* at about this time. The technique discloses considerable freedom—which in Rousseau derives from preliminary sketches—and thus provides us with an earliest possible date. On the other hand, the subject—the African theme so dear to Gérôme—suggests that the painting could hardly have been executed after 1904, when reliance upon academic painting gave way to the pressure of Rousseau's pictorial instinct.

Rousseau's last period begins with *Scouts Attacked by a Tiger (fig. 95)*, exhibited at the Salon des Indépendants in 1904. It is a typically transitional work: it still retains the need for a pattern, which is clearly recognizable in the attitudes of the horse, the tiger, and the human figures. These forms are ordered according to the laws of perspective with consummate, cold skill—the very opposite of Rousseau's natural way of seeing things. He has faithfully copied a model. By contrast, in painting the primeval forest he was guided solely by his passion for the plant world. In this respect, his later paintings are here foreshadowed. Though begun as a factitious escape into the picturesque, Rousseau turns the subject into an authentic escape: the tropical vegetation gives free rein to his imagination. The unreal takes shape. Every year hereafter, we will have one or more of the large, utterly exceptional tropical landscapes such as *Hungry Lion (colorplate, page 75)*, *The Snake Charmer (colorplate, page 97)*, and *The Dream (colorplate, page 133)*. Rousseau's powers of invention overflow in all their purity, having profited from a long experience of painting. Rousseau lets himself be carried away, and in these compact compositions achieves a space of his own—tangled and at the same time well ordered, thanks to a kind of rhythmic perspective woven by the bristling vegetation. We have a number of eyewitness accounts of how Rousseau worked in this period. Ardengo Soffici, an Italian painter, watched him working on one of his most complex exotic landscapes, *The Jungle: Tiger Attacking a Buffalo (fig. 152)*, and reports that he first painted all the greens, then the blues, then the reds. This is a strange technique, based entirely on intuition, and thereby characterized by direct, immediate, and total confidence. It helps us to understand the boldness of Rousseau's tones, both pure and mixed, invariably harmonized with the greatest appropriateness. At the same time we understand why Rousseau attached so little importance to his tropical landscapes: they came into being almost without his conscious participation. These works expressed a part of him which he himself disavowed, and he could not possibly estimate them at their real value. Between 1904 and 1910 Rousseau painted many such landscapes, but he exhibited only five of them at the Salon d'Automne and three at the Salon des Indépendants. And yet we feel that the theme interested him. He was looking for new sources of inspiration and found them in old issues of *Magasin pittoresque*. There we find engravings of rare species of animals—birds like the bird in *Merry Jesters (colorplate, page 103)*. The magazine described such a bird in one of its columns devoted to plants and animals, which Rousseau must have read eagerly. It has also been recently discovered that he owned a children's picture book with many illustrations of wild animals, some of which provided models for his monkeys, for the buffalo with crescent-shaped horns which appears in *Tiger Attacking a Buffalo*, and for the encounter depicted in *Negro Attacked by a Jaguar (fig. 167)*. This last is an interpretation of a photograph in the same book, showing an animal trainer or zoo attendant playing with a jaguar *(fig. 168)*. Similarly, the painting *The Banana Harvest (fig. 166)* seems to follow closely a contemporary illustration, but the colors—the nacreous grays, the dark greens, and the yellows—suffice to transfigure the picture and to make us forget that what Rousseau actually intended was a realistic African landscape. But now he can permit himself every liberty. He leaves his imprint on everything he touches. He can paint slowly, with care, as he does when preparing a work for exhibition, or he can paint very fast, as his technique discloses. This is the case with many landscapes: first he covered the canvas with sweeping brush strokes, and then went back over it with tiny rapid strokes. Such differences in execution indicate no more than the ultimate intention of the works and provide no clues for dating them. We know that Rousseau had been using both these modes of painting for years, and we also know that he did not shrink from treating the same subject twice—the second version being invariably the freer one.

However, the degree of liberty he takes increases with time. It can reach surprising proportions in such a painting as *Negress with Baskets (fig. 165)*, which stands out among Rousseau's works, but we possess undeniable proof that it is by his hand: a photograph of it was included among others Rousseau had taken of his canvases *(see fig. 16)*.

Most interesting of all in this period was Rousseau's spiritual liberation, and the form this liberation took. For years he had aspired to paint only in the academic manner, but now he suddenly became interested in the experiments of his contemporaries: he painted several still lifes. The most important of these, *Still Life with Coffeepot (colorplate, page 93)*, was bought from the painter by Ardengo Soffici, who also gives us its date—1907. Thus, we may group around this date the other still lifes, which Rousseau never exhibited. The genre appealed to him, he painted the still lifes for his own pleasure, and they gave him an admirable opportunity to make use of his gifts. Those were, by the way, the years when his painting was becoming increasingly more personal. It cannot be said that he gained perfect control of it, for this would presuppose a complete lucidity Rousseau never had, but the progressive liberation of his idiom and its increasingly predominant influence in his work finally usurp the role of consciousness in his art sufficiently enough to determine its development. Rousseau's investigations and solutions become more and more personal. It is enough to look at the portraits he painted at this time, especially that of Joseph Brummer *(fig. 134)*. We know what enormous difficulties Rousseau experienced with the human figure, with the mobility of features, and the articulation of the body. We know the stages he went through in perfecting his portraits, and now we witness the assertion of his style. He solves the problem of the third dimension, which had disturbed him so much, by adapting it to the surface: he transposes volumes into planes which he spreads out and organizes in relation to one another, suggesting a perception of space while avoiding its concrete figuration. Is this not a rudimentary but authentic version of the Cubist ambition to re-create volume independently of figuration, according to the requirements of the flat surface? Look at Brummer's face and observe how it is worked out, and notice the deliberate distortions Rousseau introduced into his portrait of Apollinaire *(colorplate, page 131)*, particularly in the second version *(fig. 133)*. This development leads us to assign to the same period a whole series of portraits where analogous solutions may be observed, such as the portrait of a child with a doll *(fig. 105)* and the portraits shown in figures 100–103. On the other hand, his self-portrait *(fig. 83)* and the portrait of his second wife *(fig. 84)* must be dated earlier, in my opinion. Since it is plausible that Rousseau painted the latter portrait while his wife was still alive—before 1903—and since the freedom of the brush stroke is in keeping with his sketches from nature, we are inclined to see in these two little portraits a transitional stage between the large portraits of 1895 and Rousseau's last portraits, the most famous of which is that of Apollinaire.

This extraordinary portrait is also the one about whose execution we possess the most information. We know that Rousseau used a measuring tape on his models and that he transposed the dimensions very exactly onto the canvas. We also know that he outlined his composition in charcoal and that he changed almost nothing of it later. However, he implored his models, Apollinaire and Marie Laurencin, to come and sit for him. He said that he would supply some "pretty corner in the Luxembourg" to serve as background, although actually he did not need it at all. The background he finally supplied was imaginary vegetation of the type long familiar to him. Why, after mistakenly painting gillyflowers instead of sweet williams, was he so eager to paint a second version of the portrait? I think there is only one possible reason: Rousseau was trying unconsciously to justify the plant forms dictated to him by instinct, "the pretty corner in the Luxembourg" being only an alibi. He felt the need to guarantee the veracity of the forms. Because he felt at fault, the confusion between gillyflowers and sweet williams disturbed him, and he hastened to repair his mistake. In full possession of his powers, Rousseau still had strange scruples. No painter so unsure of himself could ever be a painter like other painters.

We might go on and analyze Rousseau's works one by one in order to grasp their particularities and discover, if possible, the secret motives animating them, as well as the visible traces they contain of the painter's circumstances. In every case Rousseau's personality would emerge as we have already discerned it—incompatible with any traditional idea of the painter, at odds with all our inherited notions. To gain better insight into his singularity we have focused analysis on the works that cast the greatest light on Rousseau's approach to painting, on those works in which the act of painting summoned up all his faculties; the same faculties appear, though more isolated or attenuated, in every one of his works. In conclusion, we shall merely reaffirm the great fascination we feel today in the face of Rousseau's extraordinary achievement, discarding all preconceived ideas, concerned less for analytic niceties than for his over-all effect.

Shadow and light merge; the world has recovered its unity. Things have but *one* possible image, a single face which welcomes us and holds us. In this closed space where Rousseau's painting confines us, we are able to attain something like his own indefatigable serenity. The familiar, insurmountable split between ourselves and a crumbling world, which modern art has been reflecting now for more than half a century, is suddenly healed. Though we know this peace is provisional, almost miraculous, still what Rousseau restores to us is nothing less than an eternal human longing for a lost Eden.

Much has been said about Rousseau's naïveté, but not enough about his pictorial innocence. It is his profound candor which supplies his imagination with its strength. Whatever his intentions, he cannot but see the world in terms of the deep ties which bind him to nature, where the rational order is not distinct from the irrational, where harmony is pre-arranged and to discover it he need only follow his feeling. He is no subject, nor is the world his object, but together they form an indivisible whole.

Rousseau's painting goes beyond the individual consciousness, back to the collective impersonal roots of the human imagination, to a zone where contradictions and incompatibilities are dissolved at the birth of any really strong expression. The signification of the forms points to the archetype—first model and primordial source of value—slumbering in the depths, an affirmation of life we assent to without our knowledge. Barely evoked, it awakens into being and touches off endless repercussions as it sends us back over the painter's footsteps. Rousseau brings us face to face with wild animals, with the marvelous, with the fantastic. By whatever gate we may enter his pictorial universe, it magnetizes and revivifies.

Our reactions explain the fate of such an art. Its vogue, however great, is accounted for by the conditions of life today. As man becomes more acutely aware of his anguish, he feels increasingly that Rousseau's contribution meets an urgent need by preserving the possibility of the fullness of life. The laughter of Rousseau's contemporaries has been countered with warm appreciation in later generations. His greatness was first recognized by other artists. The form of his genius has been accepted. We regard him today as the supreme primitive, the very prototype of the artist, a perfect illustration of the relationship between art and the dream, such as Surrealism codified it.

Today, more than half a century after Rousseau's death, we can even assign his painting a place in art history. His landscapes truly achieve that solid contact with nature which the Barbizon School had spontaneously pursued in its effort to obliterate the last remnants of romantic artificiality. But the realism for which Théodore Rousseau and Daubigny had paved the way was most fully realized, strange as it may seem, by the Douanier who never intended any such thing—and at the very moment when painting was embarking on a new flight from reality. Rousseau's career as a painter coincides with the Post-Impressionist reaction. But whereas Signac and Seurat, though opposed to the evanescent forms of the Impressionists, codified the latters' fragmentation of visual reality and produced the most intellectual realism which has ever existed, Rousseau from the outset went back to realistic means of expression, as though its freshness had never been exhausted. Thus, in his own way, he took part in the reaction against Impressionism; moreover, as we have repeatedly observed, he came close to the Cubist experiments, just as in his own way he plumbed the sources of exoticism. The pictorial flight of the romantics, which degenerated into the cheap orientalism of nineteenth-century academic art, only to be transformed into a desperate gesture by Gauguin, finds its most limpid solution in Rousseau. Gauguin's flight to Tahiti, dramatizing the conflict between Western man and his environment, was not as painterly a solution as Rousseau's, though Rousseau never traveled farther than the Jardin des Plantes. He escaped into painting, his eyes wide open to the attractiveness of things, and made of art a coveted goal, his own Tahiti. And when, with the advent of the twentieth century, what had been so pompous and fatuous in the preceding century fell into oblivion, as art became simpler and profounder, Rousseau promptly came into his own. Like the influence of African masks, he helped guide modern art to new awareness and new truths which learning had obscured. At the same time he has had direct descendants—the latter-day naïve or primitive painters. Rousseau's vision, both as a whole and in detail, persists in these artists, and the same joy in painting drives them to give each thing its "finished" aspect. However, it seems that each of the best-known naïve painters has inherited but a part of Rousseau's patrimony: Vivin, the love of detail; Bombois, the powerful clarity of forms; Bauchant, the candid intellectual aspirations; and Séraphine, the visionary gifts of that man who was so fond of faraway, tropical landscapes. We follow with love the progress of all these painters, asking them to restore to us that state of grace which the Douanier revealed. We are asking to regain our paradise lost.

Paris, 1961

Rousseau's Writings

NOTE:

Rousseau wrote three plays. The first, entitled *L'Etudiant en goguettes* (The Jolly Student), seems to be a youthful work. The manuscript, at present, is in an American collection. Rousseau's two other plays, *A Visit to the 1889 Fair* (comedy in 3 acts and 10 scenes, written in 1889) and *A Russian Orphan's Revenge* (drama in 5 acts and 19 scenes, written in 1899), were published by Tristan Tzara (Éditions Pierre Cailler, Geneva, 1947).

A number of Rousseau's letters were published in *Soirées de Paris*, No. 20 (thirty-four letters to Apollinaire, one to Félix Fénéon, one to Serge Yastrebtsoff, seven to Brummer, three to Ardengo Soffici, one to André Dupont, and one to Eugénie-Léonie V.).

Six letters to Boucher, the investigating magistrate at the trial, and one letter to Pannelier, Rousseau's municipal councillor, were published by Maître Garçon in *Le Douanier Rousseau, accusé naïf* (Quatre Chemins-Éditart, Paris, 1953).

A letter to Vollard was published in the catalogue to the Rousseau exhibition at the Musée d'Art Moderne, Paris, 1944.

Rousseau's letter to the mayor of Laval was published by J. Grimod (*Le Petit Journal*, Jan. 7, 1935).

We know of five unpublished letters: three addressed to Vollard (in American collections), one to Joséphine, and one to a person unknown to us (both in Paris collections) (see note 3, page 310).

Excerpt from *A Visit to the 1889 Fair*

Comedy in 3 acts and 10 scenes

(M. and Mme Lebozeck have come from Brittany, with their maid Mariette, to see the World's Fair.)

From Act III, scene 3

A corner of the Fair at the Champ de Mars, including the Eiffel Tower, etc.

MARIETTE (*noticing the Eiffel Tower*): Ah, Holy Mother of God, ain't it lovely, ain't it beautiful—and what's that big ladder over there; it's surely taller than our church steeple! Ah, that's funny, but how can you climb up there? The bars ain't round at all, and they're all askew! Just look, people are climbing up anyway, some of them are all the way up to the top, and, by golly, they're no bigger than plant lice. How did they get there? You know, the inventors of this thing had a funny idea, it's all right, but I could have thought of something better. M. Lebozeck, won't you explain it to me; I can't make head or tail of it. How can you climb all the way up there, where the big flag is, you see? You know, if it's all right with you, we could climb up too. I'd find out what's inside that big ladder, I'm all stirred up and I want to learn about things.

MME LEBOZECK: Benjamin dear, Mariette's right, that Eiffel Tower is worth seeing. We could surely do like the others and take a look at it. It must be fun to go to the top, there must be quite a breeze up there—lots of air, and I don't mean music. So if it's all right with you, let's go over this way, we'll find out what you have to do to go up. Come on, don't you want to—surely you won't say no to your little wife?

LEBOZECK (*noticing the guard*): Hey, Mister, may I ask you something? Would you please tell me what you have to do to get to the top of that big ladder?

148

GUARD (*slightly peeved*): What d'you mean, that big ladder? Let me tell you, Monsieur, that's the Eiffel Tower, the tallest in the world, and mind you, it's 300 meters high. Where do you come from? Haven't you ever heard of it before?

LEBOZECK: You call it a tower? I always thought a tower was round, that looks like a ladder with rungs! But that isn't what I want to know. How do you get up on that tower, if that's what you call it—all the way to the top? What do we have to do?

GUARD (*showing him the entrance*): There, just go straight ahead to the ticket office; you'll see how much you have to pay and then you'll go up by the staircase or the elevator—it's the same price.

MME LEBOZECK: Well, let's go, dear, it can't cost a hundred francs. Don't be afraid, and please don't lose your temper and spoil our fun. After all, it isn't every day we come to Paris—and good heavens, since we've seen all these lovely things at the Fair, there's no point worrying about a few francs. Let's go, make up your mind, times flies, let's not waste it.

LEBOZECK: All right, woman, all right, we'll go up to the top of this famous Eiffel Tower. Here's the ticket office, and I can see from here it's five francs to go up to the top. How about it? We're going, aren't we—it's all settled?

MME LEBOZECK: Oh, how wonderful. Sure, we're going.

MARIETTE: Oh, that's real nice. Thank you, sir, thank you too, ma'am. I'm lucky to work for two nice people like you.
(*They go to the top of the Eiffel Tower and then continue their visit to the Fair, walking in the direction of the Trocadéro.*)

LEBOZECK: That was some climb, you really get hot. You'd think there'd be some way to get a glass of water, just a plain glass of water. There were restaurants on the second floor of the tower, but they looked too expensive and so we passed them by. Oh, if I could only find a drinking fountain, but I guess there's not much chance of that. I wish there was one, though; I can't go on much longer. I tell you, my tongue's hanging out.

MME LEBOZECK: Now, now, Benjamin dear, be patient. We're in the mood for a nice walk today. If it's all the same to you, I say we should go across this bridge. There seem to be lots of interesting things over there—beehives, for instance, and an aquarium full of fishes, and then the Trocadéro, that beautiful monument you see right ahead of you. Let's go over there—what do you say?

MARIETTE: But ma'am, there's also the Invalides. They say you mustn't miss it. Someone back home told me there's a man there with a wooden head, that ought to be fun, I'd like to see that. If it's not too far, we might go there. And then there are also the Arabisques or Amarmites, I don't know what you call 'em, but it always ends with that word. We're not going to miss all that, are we? It'll be lots of fun, I'm sure, O-ooh, I'm excited already.

LEBOZECK: Well, now we're here, we ought to make the most of it. As Zéphyrine suggested, let's take a look at that beautiful monument in front of us. Then we'll go take a ride on one of those little boats going by right now. That big river is called the Seine; we must see that too.

MARIETTE: O-ooh, Monsieur, that's a good idea; now we're here we mustn't miss any of it. But there's so many things, I don't see how we can get it all in, in the little time we've got left in the capital.

MME LEBOZECK: Let's go inside the Trocadéro since we're here; let's follow the crowds that are going up to the second floor. Look, Benjamin dear, you see it was a good idea we came here—it's just like being back in Ploërmel. Oh look! Over there! There's the bride getting ready for the big moment. See the groom with his bouquet and then the mother and father all dressed up. You'd think they were real, wouldn't you, Benjamin, wouldn't you, Mariette? And the table with the hollows for the plates, and the big fireplace with the buckwheat pancakes on the stove! Really, it's just like home. Ah, there are men and women, too, but they're not like the ones at home!

LEBOZECK: Zéphyrine, my sweet, that's because they're from other places.

MARIETTE: But those poor people must be awful tired standing around like that all day long. I sure wouldn't like to have to stand here like that, perfectly still.

LEBOZECK: You silly goose, those people aren't alive! What a silly girl! They're made out of wax—just take a good look. You don't think they could stand like that without ever moving if they were real, do you? Keep your eyes open, for you'll find more of them wherever we go. But nowhere to get a drink of water! That's one thing they sure haven't been lavish with. Why, we haven't even been to see the big boulevards yet, and I'm dying of thirst.

MME LEBOZECK: But darling, just a minute ago by the bridge I saw a man selling some kind of yellowish liquid in glasses, and there was some kind of reddish liquid, too. I forget what he was calling it. If you like, we could all go back and have some. Why don't we?

LEBOZECK: Oh, it's not worth going back for. Anyway, I bet it isn't very good. Let's keep on going and maybe we'll find a public fountain.

MARIETTE: Yes, yes, let's keep on going. I want to see some more. How about the Invalides I was just telling you about? Let's cross back over the river, it isn't far. At the same time we can see everything on the other bank, there, along the boulevard. There's a little train, isn't that sweet, a tiny baby train? See the engine and the coaches, a teeny-weeny train.

MME LEBOZECK: Oh yes, Mariette, let's go over there. Doesn't it look lovely! Oh, but look over there. The barrel! What a big one! Hurry up, everyone, maybe they're selling cider! If it isn't too expensive, I'd be glad to drink a glass or two.

MARIETTE: Oh ma'am, wouldn't that be nice? Can't you just taste our good Brittany cider! I'm very much afraid we won't find any of that here. But I'm ready for whatever you decide.

LEBOZECK: Patience, patience, we'll be back in our dear Brittany soon enough and then we'll have a real treat, pancakes and everything.

MARIETTE: What's that over there? All shiny and it looks pretty big. Oh, I want to see what that is.

LEBOZECK: What are you talking about? I don't see nothing like that over there. Not shiny, anyway. There are women with hats like umbrellas, and they're dragging little carts behind them. What can these people be?

MME LEBOZECK: Look at those women. Why, their hair is braided, just like the girls at home, and it goes way down their backs. No, their skin isn't white. Funny, they must be cannibals.

A VOICE: They're Annamites!

MARIETTE: Oh, that's it! I didn't hear right before: Dynamites or Amarmites I thought it was. Anyhow, I sure wouldn't like to be as ugly as those women, I'd never dare go out if I looked liked that.

MME LEBOZECK: They sure are ugly. How can their husbands love them? It's just not possible they could have husbands.

A VOICE: Those aren't women, they're men, so be careful.

MARIETTE: Oh no! Isn't that a scream! I sure wouldn't want to marry a man like that. Dear me, no! They're sure not very handsome, are they, those Aramites?

LEBOZECK: And how about you, Zéphyrine? Wouldn't you like me to wear a big tail like that down my back and shave off my mustache? Wouldn't you like that?

MME LEBOZECK: No, Benjamin dear, I wouldn't like that. I wouldn't like you at all if you looked like those fellows. You're not so handsome, it's true, but you're better looking than they are.

MARIETTE: Oh, come on! There's that shiny thing I saw in the distance. Come on, let's see what it is.

LEBOZECK: So that's what it is. Just a piece of cannon like on warships and around seaports. Haven't you ever seen one before, my girl? Haven't you ever been to Brest and seen one of those big ships that go on long voyages and fight battles? Whew! A thing like that's no joke, you know. One of those things could kill you.

MME LEBOZECK: That's probably how my brother died, fighting some battle out there in Tonkin, poor boy. Why did he have to go out there and get himself killed like that—after all the sacrifices our poor parents made for him? Such a sad thing, the military profession, though I don't know why they call it a profession. Oh dear, all that killing. Nobody deserves to be killed like that. My poor brother! *(She sobs.)*

MARIETTE: O-ooh, yes. That's cannon, all right, big ones, too. They sure look like they could kill people, I bet if you filled those big openings with powder and shot, they'd destroy anything that got in their way. Oh, war, war, what a terrible thing!

Excerpt from *A Russian Orphan's Revenge*

Drama in 5 acts and 19 scenes

(Sophie has run away with Henri from her native Russia, leaving her aunt Yadwigha, who was opposed to their marriage. The two lovers arrive in Brussels, where Henri meets his friend Édouard.)

From Act III, scene 2

A room in the Hôtel de France. Henri, Sophie, and Édouard are seated at a lavishly spread table.

HENRI *(to Sophie)*: My dear Sophie, you must be hungry. I have ordered the best wines and the best dishes for this meal, so that you may keep a good memory of this happy day, and so that our friend Édouard will not think us inhospitable.

SOPHIE: Your kindness doesn't surprise me, Henri, coming as it does from you. You are always the perfect gentleman. Never fear—I'll do justice to the dinner, that walk this afternoon gave me a rather good appetite. I hope you and your friend feel the same way about it.
(Henri and Édouard nod in agreement. Sophie rings the bell. A waiter brings in the first course and serves it.)

WAITER *(aside)*: And this is only the beginning. They look like hearty eaters to me. Where in the world do they come from, I wonder, ordering so much to eat for three persons. Ah, now I've got it: they've been traveling and couldn't find a place to eat all day, so they're making up for it now. This will go on all night. Ah, me, what a profession—what a profession to have to wait on people.

(Sophie, Henri, and Édouard begin to eat.)

HENRI: I see I chose the right place. Everything is excellent. Doesn't it taste good—especially in such pleasant company. How do you find it, dear Sophie?

SOPHIE: Oh you're quite right. The food is exquisite. You can see I'm doing justice to it.

ÉDOUARD: You'd think I was starved. I haven't had a meal as good as this in a long time.

HENRI: We'll finish it off with a few glasses of champagne to celebrate our forthcoming marriage and to toast our friend Édouard's health.

(They clink their glasses of champagne and toast each other. Henri rises from the table to see Édouard out.)

HENRI *(to Édouard)*: My dear friend, I am very happy to have run across you here. It is probable that I'll soon be asking you to do me a great favor.

ÉDOUARD: I am entirely at your disposal. Let me know the moment you need me. *(Exit)*

(Henri goes back to the table and sits down next to Sophie.)

HENRI: At last we're alone, dear Sophie, quite alone! I'm so happy, now that I can look at you and admire your beauty. My, but you're pretty tonight! Your cheeks are just delicately flushed, your big beautiful eyes are lit up with an inner sparkle, and your bosom is throbbing as your heart beats faster. How I love you like this, dearest one, how lovely you are! Nowhere have I ever found a woman who could match you in any respect. Burning desire is taking possession of me, yes, desire to embrace you tenderly. I beg of you, my beloved, let me kiss those pink cheeks so alive with youth and beauty, do let me! *(He moves closer to Sophie, trying to put his arm around her waist.)*

SOPHIE *(rising from her seat)*: Monsieur, what are you doing? It seems to me that you are not behaving properly. Your conduct is clumsy and rude. If you love me as much as you say, you ought to respect my person. I must ask you to control yourself better than that in the future.

HENRI (*also rising*): You call it rudeness, that I am burning with love for you? That I cannot sleep at night, no, not a wink, struggling against the wicked thoughts that assail me? No, I don't deserve to be treated this way. I may have failed to control myself, but I'm suffering, I'm losing my mind, alas! a thousand things are rushing through my brain. Oh my Sophie, my beloved, you are my one and only, the one on whom I have pinned all my hopes. Don't treat me so cruelly! Let me be near you, don't send me away. Every fiber in my heart is breaking. I love you, my dear, I adore you. Please, let me have an answer to my appeal, I implore you on my bended knee. (*He throws himself at her feet.*) Here I am at your feet imploring your forgiveness. My love for you makes me cling to you like this, like ivy around those age-old oak trees, which can only be separated from them by incredible force. My love for you is responsible for this momentary aberration, my love for you made me disrespectful. Forgive me, dear Sophie, let me place one little kiss on your pretty white hands. I love you, Sophie! My life, my whole being, belongs to you.

(*Sophie extends her right hand and he kisses it.*)

Oh thank you, Sophie dear, thank you. One little kiss is little enough, I suppose, but it makes me the happiest of men. I couldn't be as happy as I am now if someone gave me millions of francs. How beautiful you are, my beloved. Oh yes, you are beautiful; an air of majesty reigns everywhere in your lovely person.

(*Sophie tells him to get up. He seats himself by her side and continues:*)

Dear Sophie, you whom I have chosen for my life's companion, to share with me the ups and downs of life, your charms could hardly be expected not to have conquered my whole being. Let me look into your eyes, let me touch that lovely long hair which is so becoming to you, let me kiss this mouth which once told me "I love you," and did not lie. Oh, let me, let me press you to my bursting heart. My brain is on fire, I don't know what is going on inside me, I am shivering all over. Oh, Sophie, my beautiful one, my beloved, don't make me go through the tortures of the damned—I adore you! No, I can't stand it any longer, this fever which oppresses me, this desire which is burning and gripping my whole being. (*He moves closer to her and embraces her tenderly.*) Sophie, darling Sophie, be mine as I am yours!

(*They slowly get up, and Sophie leans her head on Henri's shoulder. They walk slowly out of the room. Curtain.*)

HENRI (*alone in the café of the Hôtel de France*): At last she has yielded to me, and it was not easy, that child. She really thought I was going to marry her, imagine it, a girl without a dowry, without a future. What the devil made her think I would ever be her husband? I, her husband! (*He sneers.*) With my good record as a bank clerk? Those are the things that matter. I'd be stupid to tie myself down to a girl like that. Thank you, no! She hasn't a penny—what good could she be to me? Penniless! No, I'll never go through with the marriage, I won't commit such a blunder. Not that she isn't pretty and full of charm, but that's all. Beauty isn't money. Ah, Money, Money, the great god Money! Nothing is greater than that—just seeing it spread out on a table I can't take my eyes away. What is more lovely than the clear ring of those twenty-franc pieces called louis d'or? What a beautiful sound! Oh, Money, god of the whole world whom everyone worships, so often the cause of every crime and contemptible action, I can never adore you and cherish you enough. Money, lovely Money, don't ever leave me—you are worth more than all the women in the world. But come to think of it, what am I doing sitting around here? There is no longer any reason. While that foolish Sophie is resting, I can be getting away from this place. I shall make myself scarce now—like a little bird I'll silently steal away.

Plates

25 Rousseau's Self-Portrait, 1884   26 Portrait of Rousseau's First Wife, 1884

27   *Tollhouse, Quai d'Auteuil, 1885*   28   *Quai d'Auteuil, 1885*

29   *The Village*, 1886

30   *Landscape with Fisherman*, after 1886

51   *The Orchard,* after 1886

32 *Landscape with Cows*, 1895–97

33 *Oval Landscape*, 1886

34 *The Promenade*, between 1886 and 1890

35 *Carnival Evening*, exhibited in 1886

36   *The Canal (Landscape with Tree Trunks),* about 1887

37   *Riverbank*, 1887

38 Pen drawing

59   Pencil drawing

40   *Rendezvous in the Forest*, between 1886 and 1890

41   *Walk in the Forest*, between 1886 and 1890

42　*Family* (perhaps exhibited in 1891 as *The M. Family*)

43 *Present and Past.* Painted before
1890, this picture was repainted at
the time of Rousseau's second marriage, after 1899

Along with the painting was the
following verse:
Separated from one another
From all those whom they had loved
They are united anew,
Faithful always in thought.

44   Pencil drawing. Probably study for the lost painting *Le dîner sur l'herbe*, exhibited in 1888

45   *Portrait of a Young Girl,* about 1890

46 Pencil drawing

47 Pencil drawing

48 *Portrait of Pierre Loti*, 1891–92 (repainted about 1910)

49   *Poet's Flowers*, about 1890

Bonne Fête
15 Aout 92

50   *Happy Anniversary*, 1892

51 *Vase of Flowers,* about 1893

52 *Vase of Flowers,* about 1893

53   Pencil drawing

54   *Transatlantic Liner in a Storm (Storm at Sea)*, 1890–93

55   *The Carmagnole*, 1893

56   Detail of *The Carmagnole*

57   *View of the Pont de Grenelle,* 1892

58   *View of Gentilly Seen from the Bièvre,* before 1895

59 *Landscape, Outskirts of Paris,* about 1895

60   Study for *Path in Parc Montsouris*, 1895

61   *Path in Parc Montsouris*, exhibited in 1895

62   *The Mill,* about 1896

63 *Landscape at Pontoise*, 1896

64   Study for *View of the Fortifications*, 1896

65   *View of the Fortifications*, exhibited in 1896

66   *View of the Fortifications,* about 1910

67 *Farmyard*, 1896–98

68   *View of the Bois de Boulogne*, 1896–98

69   *Portrait of a Woman*, 1895

70   *Portrait of a Woman*, 1897

71   Pencil drawing, 1901

72   *Unpleasant Surprise*, exhibited in 1901

73　*Landscape : The Fortifications*, between 1890 and 1905

74 *The Painter and His Model,* between 1900 and 1905

75   *Innocence*, by Léon Gérôme, 1852

76   *Happy Quartet (Adam and Eve)* . exhibited in 1902

77 *Landscape*, about 1902–03

78   *Landscape at Charenton*, about 1902–03

79   *Spring: View of Alfortville,* 1902

80   *Surburb: Banks of the Marne*, about 1905

81   Study for *House in Paris Suburb*, 1902

82 *House in Paris Suburb,* 1902

83   *Self-Portrait with Oil Lamp,* 1902–03

84   *Portrait of Rousseau's Second Wife with Oil Lamp*, 1902–03

85   *The Lion of Belfort* (study), before 1904

86   *Landscape with the Moulin d'Alfort,* before 1904

87 *Landscape with Factory,* about 1904

88   *The Footbridge at Passy*, about 1904

89   Study for *View of the Eiffel Tower*, about 1904

90   *View of the Eiffel Tower,* about 1904

91   *View of Saint-Cloud from the Heights of Bellevue,* about 1904

92   *Spring in the Valley of the Bièvre*, about 1904

93 Detail of the painting *Cockfight*, by Léon Gérôme

94 Detail of *Woman Walking in a Tropical Forest* (fig. 96)

95   *Scouts Attacked by a Tiger*, exhibited in 1904

96   *Woman Walking in a Tropical Forest*, 1905

97   *Woman in Red in the Forest*, after 1905

98   *Country Wedding*, exhibited in 1905

99 *Representatives of Foreign Powers Come to Salute the Republic as a Peaceful Gesture*, exhibited in 1907

100   *Portrait of a Man,* about 1905

101 *Portrait of a Woman*, about 1905

102 *Portrait of a Man, 1906*

103   *Portrait of a Woman, 1906*

104   *Portrait of a Baby*, probably painted after 1905 (The picture has been lost; this is a photograph that belonged to the artist and bears the title written in by him)

105 *Child with Doll*, 1908

106   *Road in Repair* (study), about 1906

107 *View of the Outskirts of Paris,* about 1906

108   Study for *Landscape with Cow*, 1906

109   *Landscape with Cow (View of the Outskirts of Paris, Commune of Bagneux)*, about 1906

110　*Meadow*, about 1906

111   *Meadow, Banks of the Oise*, 1907

112   *Breton Scene (Summer)* (first version), 1906

113   *Farm at Bannalec (Breton Landscape)*, by
Camille Bernier. On two occasions Rousseau was inspired by this picture, which
was in the Museum of Fine Arts, at Angers

114 *Breton Scene* (*Summer*) (second version), probably exhibited in 1907

115 Study for *View of the Pont de Sèvres*, 1908

116 Photograph of *View of the Pont de Sèvres*, which Rousseau had taken before adding the airplane and the dirigible (see also colorplate, page 113)

117 *Srollers in a Park*, 1907–08

118 *Landscape with the Dirigible "Patrie" and a Biplane*, 1907–08

119 The dirigible *Patrie*. Such ailerons had never before been used on a dirigible, nor had they been fully installed during the test flights. They were used for the first time in 1907

20 *Fishermen*, 1908

121 Study for *Landscape with the Dirigible "Patrie,"* 1907–08

22 *Landscape with the Dirigible "Patrie," 1907–08*

123   *Landscape with Ruins,* about 1906

124   *Autumn: View of Damery-Boursault*, about 1907

125   *Winter Landscape,* 1907

126   *The Pink Candle*, 1907

127 Pencil drawing

128   *Still Life (with Cherries)*, 1908

129   Pencil drawing

130   Pencil drawing

131   *Rabbit Feeding*, 1908

152   *Eve*, after 1904

153　*The Muse Inspiring the Poet* (second version), 1909

134   *Portrait of Joseph Brummer*, exhibited in 1909

135   *The Tiger Hunt*, before 1904

136   *Père Juniet's Cart*, 1908

137   Photograph of the Juniet family.
Collection James Johnson Sweeney

138 Study for *View of Parc Montsouris*, about 1909

139   *View of Parc Montsouris,* about 1909

140   *View of Saint-Cloud,* after 1905

141 *The Fisherman*, about 1909

142   *The Walk*, about 1908

145 *Path in the Woods*, 1909

144   Study, 1908–10

145 Study for *Avenue in the Park of Saint-Cloud* (see frontispiece)

146   *View of the Chair Factory and the Quai de Seine at Alfortville,* 1897

147 *The Chair Factory and the Quai de Seine at Alfortville*, 1909

148 *Landscape* (study), about 1909

149 *Fishermen*, 1909

150   *Jungle with a Lion*, after 1904

151 *Flamingos*, 1907

152   *The Jungle: Tiger Attacking a Buffalo*, 1908

153   *Tiger and Buffalo Fighting*, 1909–10

154   *Tropical Landscape*, 1909

155   *The Jungle: Monkeys with Oranges*, 1908

156 *The Tropics (Monkeys in the Jungle)*, about 1910

157 *Exotic Landscape: Ape and Indian*, 1910

158   *The Waterfall*, 1910

159   *In the Luxembourg Gardens*

160   *View of Parc Montsouris,* about 1910

161   Study for *View from the Pont d'Austerlitz*, about 1910

162 *View from the Pont d'Austerlitz*, about 1910

163   *Landscape*, about 1910

164 *Woman with Basket of Eggs*, about 1910

165   *Negress with Baskets (Basket Weaver)*,1910

166 *The Banana Harvest*, 1910

167   *Negro Attacked by a Jaguar*, about 1909

168   Page from a picture book of wild animals that belonged to Rousseau

169 *Horse Attacked by a Jaguar,* about 1910

170   *Tropical Forest with Monkeys*, 1910

171   *Exotic Landscape*, 1910

172　*Two Monkeys in the Jungle*, 1910

175   *Monkeys in the Jungle*, 1910

174   *Vase of Flowers* (first version), about 1909 (see also colorplate, page 121)

175 *Vase of Flowers*, 1909–10

176 *Vase of Flowers*, 1909–10

177 *Vase of Flowers*, 1910

178   *Flowers in a White Vase,* 1910

179   *Vase of Flowers*, 1910

See figure 35

See figure 41

See figure 96

See figure 97

180 Development of Rousseau's style

See figure 29

See figure 32

See figure 108

See figure 109

See figure 110

See figure 111

181   How Rousseau developed a subject

List of Works Illustrated

305

BLACK-AND-WHITE ILLUSTRATIONS

31 *The Orchard*. After 1886. Oil on canvas, $14^5/_8 \times 21^1/_4''$. Collection Georges Renand, Paris

32 *Landscape with Cows*. 1895–97. Oil on canvas, $20 \times 26''$. Philadelphia Museum of Art (Louise and Walter Arensberg Collection)

33 *Oval Landscape*. 1886. Oil on canvas, $14^5/_8 \times 18^1/_8''$. Carstairs Gallery, New York

34 *The Promenade*. Between 1886 and 1890. Oil on canvas, $18^1/_8 \times 21^5/_8''$. Private collection, Basel

35 *Carnival Evening*. Exhibited in 1886. Oil on canvas, $43^7/_8 \times 34^1/_4''$. Philadelphia Museum of Art (Louis E. Stern Collection)

36 *The Canal (Landscape with Tree Trunks)*. 1887. Oil on canvas, $20^1/_2 \times 49''$. Barnes Foundation, Merion, Pennsylvania

37 *Riverbank*. 1887. Oil on canvas, $8^1/_4 \times 15^3/_8''$. Collection E. Tappenbeck, Paris

38 Pen drawing. Ex-collection Herbert von Garvens, Hanover

39 Pencil drawing

40 *Rendezvous in the Forest*. Between 1886 and 1890. Oil on canvas, $35^3/_8 \times 27^5/_8''$. Collection the Hon. and Mrs. Averell Harriman

41 *Walk in the Forest*. Between 1886 and 1890. Oil on canvas, $28 \times 23^5/_8''$. Kunsthaus, Zurich

42 *Family* (perhaps exhibited in 1891 as *The M. Family*). Oil on canvas, $18^1/_4 \times 21^3/_4''$. Barnes Foundation, Merion, Pennsylvania

43 *Present and Past*. Before 1890–after 1899. Oil on canvas, $33^1/_8 \times 18^1/_2''$. Barnes Foundation, Merion, Pennsylvania

44 Pencil drawing. About 1888. Ex-collection S. Yastrebtzoff

45 *Portrait of a Young Girl*. About 1890. Oil on canvas, $24 \times 17^7/_8''$. Philadelphia Museum of Art

46 Pencil drawing. $5 \times 2^3/_4''$. Collection Giorgio Morandi, Bologna

47 Pencil drawing. Private collection

48 *Portrait of Pierre Loti*. 1891–92 (repainted about 1910). Oil on canvas, $24 \times 19^5/_8''$. Kunsthaus, Zurich

49 *Poet's Flowers*. About 1890. Oil on canvas, $14^7/_8 \times 17^3/_4''$. Private collection

50 *Happy Anniversary*. 1892. Oil on canvas. Collection Charles Laughton, London

51 *Vase of Flowers*. About 1893. Oil on canvas, $24 \times 19^1/_2''$. The Tate Gallery, London

52 *Vase of Flowers*. About 1893. Oil on canvas, $21^3/_4 \times 18''$. Barnes Foundation, Merion, Pennsylvania

53 Pencil drawing. Ex-collection S. Yastrebtzoff

54 *Transatlantic Liner in a Storm (Storm at Sea)*. 1890–93. Oil on canvas, $23^5/_8 \times 28''$. Collection Mme Jean Guival

55 *The Carmagnole*. 1893. Oil on canvas, $8 \times 29^1/_2''$. Collection Dr. and Mrs. Frank Conroy

56 Detail of *The Carmagnole*

57 *View of the Pont de Grenelle*. 1892. Oil on canvas, $8 \times 29^1/_2''$. Collection Mme Goldschmidt Rothschild, Paris

58 *View of Gentilly Seen from the Bièvre*. Before 1895. Oil on canvas. Private collection

59 *Landscape, Outskirts of Paris*. About 1895. Oil on canvas, $15 \times 18^1/_8''$. The Cleveland Museum of Art

60 Study for *Path in Parc Montsouris*. 1895. Oil on canvas, $10^1/_4 \times 7^7/_8''$. Private collection, Paris

61 *Path in Parc Montsouris*. Exhibited in 1895. Oil on canvas, $29^3/_4 \times 18^1/_2''$. Private collection, New York

62 *The Mill*. About 1896. Oil on canvas, $13 \times 21^5/_8''$. Private collection

63 *Landscape at Pontoise*. 1896. Oil on canvas, $15^3/_4 \times 11^3/_4''$. Collection Mrs. William Hale Harkness, New York

64 Study for *View of the Fortifications*. 1896. Oil on canvas. Private collection

65 *View of the Fortifications* (first version). Exhibited in 1896. Oil on canvas, $18^1/_8 \times 21^5/_8''$. Private collection

66 *View of the Fortifications*. About 1910. Oil on canvas, $13 \times 16^1/_8''$. Pushkin Museum of Fine Arts, Moscow

67 *Farmyard*. 1896–98. Oil on canvas, $9^1/_2 \times 13''$. Collection Mme Nina Kandinsky, Paris

68 *View of the Bois de Boulogne*. 1896–98. Oil on canvas, $13 \times 16^1/_8''$. Ex-collection Hans Siemens

69 *Portrait of a Woman*. 1895. Oil on canvas, $59 \times 39^3/_8''$. Collection Pablo Picasso, France

70 *Portrait of a Woman*. 1897. Oil on canvas, $78^3/_4 \times 45^1/_4''$. Ex-collection Gourgaud, Paris

71 Pencil drawing. 1901

72 *Unpleasant Surprise*. Exhibited in 1901. Oil on canvas, $76^1/_2 \times 50^3/_4''$. Barnes Foundation, Merion, Pennsylvania

73 *Landscape: The Fortifications*. Between 1890 and 1905. Oil on canvas, $15^3/_8 \times 18^1/_8''$. Collection E. G. Bührle, Zurich

74 *The Painter and His Model*. Between 1900 and 1905. Oil on canvas, $22 \times 25^5/_8''$. Collection Mme Nina Kandinsky, Paris

75 *Innocence*, by Léon Gérôme. 1852. Oil on canvas. Musée de Tarbes

76 *Happy Quartet (Adam and Eve)*. Exhibited in 1902. Oil on canvas, $37 \times 22^1/_2''$. Collection the Hon. and Mrs. John Hay Whitney, New York

122 *Landscape with the Dirigible "Patrie."* 1907–08. Oil on canvas, $17^3/_4 \times 22''$. Ex-collection S. Yastrebtzoff

123 *Landscape with Ruins.* About 1906. Oil on canvas, $13 \times 16^1/_2''$. Collection Dr. and Mrs. Norman F. Laskey, Mount Kisco, New York

124 *Autumn: View of Damery-Boursault.* About 1907. Oil on canvas, $15^3/_4 \times 20^1/_2''$. Private collection, Paris

125 *Winter Landscape.* 1907. Oil on canvas, $15^3/_4 \times 20^1/_2''$. Private collection, Paris

126 *The Pink Candle.* 1907. Oil on canvas, $16^1/_4 \times 8^1/_2''$. Phillips Collection, Washington, D. C.

127 Pencil drawing. Private collection

128 *Still Life (with Cherries).* 1908. Oil on wood, $3 \times 5^1/_2''$. Collection Mrs. Max Weber

129 Pencil drawing. $4 \times 2^1/_4''$. Collection Giorgio Morandi, Bologna

130 Pencil drawing. $3^3/_4 \times 1^7/_8''$. Collection Giorgio Morandi, Bologna

131 *Rabbit Feeding.* 1908. Oil on canvas, $21^1/_4 \times 25^5/_8''$. Barnes Foundation, Merion, Pennsylvania

132 *Eve.* After 1904. Oil on canvas, $23^5/_8 \times 18^1/_8''$. Kunsthalle, Hamburg

133 *The Muse Inspiring the Poet* (second version). 1909. Oil on canvas, $51^5/_8 \times 38^1/_8''$. Pushkin Museum of Fine Arts, Moscow. (For first version see colorplate, page 131.)

134 *Portrait of Joseph Brummer.* Exhibited in 1909. Oil on canvas, $46^1/_8 \times 34^1/_4''$. Private collection

135 *The Tiger Hunt.* Before 1904. Oil on canvas, $15 \times 18^1/_8''$. The Columbus Gallery of Fine Arts, Columbus, Ohio

136 *Père Juniet's Cart.* 1908. Oil on canvas, $38^1/_8 \times 50^3/_4''$. Collection Mme Jean Walter, Paris

138 Study for *View of Parc Montsouris.* About 1909. Oil on canvas, $7^7/_8 \times 10^1/_4''$. Private collection

139 *View of Parc Montsouris.* About 1909. Oil on canvas, $25^1/_2 \times 31^1/_2''$. Barnes Foundation, Merion, Pennsylvania

140 *View of Saint-Cloud.* After 1905. Oil on canvas, $8^1/_2 \times 10^5/_8''$. Collection A. Hahnloser, Winterthur

141 *The Fisherman.* About 1909. Oil on canvas, $14^5/_8 \times 18^1/_2''$. Collection Dr. and Mrs. Harry Bakwin, New York

142 *The Walk.* About 1908. Oil on canvas, $18^1/_8 \times 15^3/_8''$. Ex-collection A. Vollard

143 *Path in the Woods.* 1909. Oil on canvas, $23^1/_2 \times 18^7/_8''$. Collection Mrs. Henry D. Sharpe, Providence, Rhode Island

144 Study. 1908–10. Oil on cardboard

145 Study for *Avenue in the Park of Saint-Cloud.* Oil on cardboard, $4^3/_4 \times 3^7/_8''$. Private collection. (For final version, see frontispiece.)

146 *View of the Chair Factory and the Quai de Seine at Alfortville.* 1897. Oil on canvas, $28^3/_4 \times 36^1/_4''$. Collection Mme Jean Walter, Paris

147 *The Chair Factory and the Quai de Seine at Alfortville.* 1909. Oil on canvas, $15 \times 18^1/_8''$. Collection Mme Jean Walter, Paris

148 *Landscape* (study). About 1909. Oil on cardboard, $9^1/_2 \times 7^1/_8''$. Ex-collection Wilhelm Uhde

149 *Fishermen.* 1909. Oil on canvas, $18^1/_8 \times 21^1/_2''$. Barnes Foundation, Merion, Pennsylvania

150 *Jungle with a Lion.* After 1904. Oil on canvas, $15^1/_8 \times 18^1/_4''$. The Museum of Modern Art, New York

151 *Flamingos.* 1907. Oil on canvas, $45^1/_4 \times 63^3/_4''$. Collection Mr. and Mrs. Charles S. Payson, New York

152 *The Jungle: Tiger Attacking a Buffalo.* 1908. Oil on canvas, $67^3/_4 \times 75^3/_8''$. The Cleveland Museum of Art

153 *Tiger and Buffalo Fighting.* 1909–10. Oil on canvas, $18^1/_8 \times 21^5/_8''$. Pushkin Museum of Fine Arts, Moscow

154 *Tropical Landscape.* 1909. Oil on canvas, $55^1/_4 \times 51''$. The National Gallery of Art, Washington, D. C. (Chester Dale Collection)

155 *The Jungle: Monkeys with Oranges.* 1908. Oil on canvas, $45^1/_4 \times 34^7/_8''$. Private collection, New York

156 *The Tropics (Monkeys in the Jungle).* About 1910. Oil on canvas, $43^3/_4 \times 63^3/_4''$. Collection Miss Adelaide Milton de Groot

157 *Exotic Landscape: Ape and Indian.* 1910. Oil on canvas, $43^1/_4 \times 61^3/_4''$. Private collection, Chicago

158 *The Waterfall.* 1910. Oil on canvas, $45^5/_8 \times 59''$. The Art Institute of Chicago (Helen Birch Bartlett Memorial Collection)

159 *In the Luxembourg Gardens.* Pencil drawing. Private collection

160 *View of Parc Montsouris.* About 1910. Oil on canvas, $15^7/_8 \times 11^3/_4''$. Private collection

161 Study for *View from the Pont d'Austerlitz.* About 1910. Oil on cardboard, $10^5/_8 \times 8^5/_8''$. Private collection

162 *View from the Pont d'Austerlitz.* About 1910. Oil on canvas, $9^1/_2 \times 7^1/_2''$. Ex-collection Mendelssohn-Bartholdy, Berlin

163 *Landscape.* About 1910. Oil on canvas, $18^1/_8 \times 18^7/_8''$. Pushkin Museum of Fine Arts, Moscow

164 *Woman with Basket of Eggs.* About 1910. Oil on canvas, $13 \times 11''$. Barnes Foundation, Merion, Pennsylvania

165 *Negress with Baskets.* 1910. Oil on canvas, $7^1/_8 \times 9^1/_8''$. Ex-collection Paul Guillaume

NOTES

1. In his book, *La Vérité sur le Douanier Rousseau* (Paris, 1961), Mr. H. Certigny ascribes to the *Portrait of Pierre Loti* certain facts (pp. 255 ff.) that can only apply to another portrait which Loti had, by his own account, destroyed in 1911. Since we know that Rousseau often returned, after many years, to the same motifs (and we have cited several instances), the fact that we learn of another, analogous canvas does not enlighten us at all about this portrait of Pierre Loti.

2. The composition, technique, and "touch" of the *Portrait of a Young Girl (La Jeune Fille en rose)* rule out any possibility that this picture was painted in 1907, as Mr. Certigny believes. In his above-mentioned book (p. 283), he seems to have taken certain information too literally. That the person who recognizes herself in this portrait, in 1961, actually posed for Rousseau in 1907, we have no doubt; but the portrait that he did of her—and which her family sold in 1919— is not the *Portrait of a Young Girl* in the Philadelphia Museum.

3. The three letters to Vollard and the letter to Joséphine have been published in *Art de France*, II, 1962.

Works Exhibited at the Salon des Indépendants 1886—1910

1886

Second Salon: August 21–September 21. Rue des Tuileries, Building B.

Four paintings exhibited:

Thunder, Left Bank of the Seine near Vanves
View of the Pont-du-Jour (Sunset)
Carnival Evening
Waiting

1887

Third Salon: March 26–May 3. Pavilion of the City of Paris, Champs-Elysées.

Three paintings exhibited:

View of the Quai d'Orsay (Autumn)
A Poor Devil
View of a Path in the Tuileries (Spring)

1888

Fourth Salon: March 23–May 3. Pavilion of the City of Paris, Champs-Elysées.

Five paintings and several drawings exhibited:

The Departure
After the Banquet
View of the Ile Saint-Louis from Pont Saint-Nicolas (Evening)
View of the Bois de Boulogne (Sunset)
Le dîner sur l'herbe

1889

Fifth Salon: September 3–October 4. Société d'Horticulture, 84 boulevard Saint-Germain.

Three paintings exhibited:

Portrait of Mlle Lepallier
The Suicide
Portrait of Mme G.

1890

Sixth Salon: March 20–April 27. Pavilion of the City of Paris, Champs-Elysées.

Five paintings and several drawings exhibited:

Myself: Portrait-Landscape
View of Issy (Impression of springtime after the storm)
View of Billancourt and Bas-Meudon (Impression of fog)
Portrait of M. B.
My First, [Portrait] of Julia Rousseau, Paris

1891

Seventh Salon: March 20–April 27. Pavilion of the City of Paris, Champs-Elysées.

Seven paintings and several drawings exhibited:

Surprised! (Storm in the Forest)
View of the Bois de Boulogne (Spring)

View of Malakoff
View of the Footbridge at Passy
Portrait of M. B.
Portrait of M. L.
The M. Family

1892

Eighth Salon: March 19–April 27. Pavilion of the City of Paris, Champs-Elysées.

Five paintings and one drawing exhibited:

The Centenary of Independence
Portrait of Mlle Jeanne (owned by M. B.)
Portrait of Mme L.
View of the Port of Bas-Meudon, after the Rain
View of the Pont de Grenelle (Trocadéro)
Longshoremen (drawing owned by my friend Claude Goubot)

1893

Ninth Salon: March 18–April 27. Pavilion of the City of Paris, Champs-Elysées.

Five paintings exhibited:

The Last Man of the 51st
Freedom
Rue de Vanves, after the Rain
View of the Ile Saint-Louis during the Night of the Fire at the Bus Depot, Quai de l'Estrapade
Portrait of M. B.

1894

Tenth Salon: April 7–May 27. Palais des Arts Libéraux, Champ-de-Mars.

Four paintings exhibited:

War
Decorative Panel (The Carmagnole)
Portrait of a Child
Portrait of M. J.

1895

Eleventh Salon: April 9–May 26. Palais des Arts Libéraux, Champ-de-Mars.

Ten paintings exhibited:

Portrait of Mme A. J. (Portrait of Alfred Jarry)
Portrait of Mme L.
Portrait of M. B.
Portrait of a Child
View of the Footbridge at Passy
View of an Arch of the Pont de Sèvres
View of Saint-Cloud from the Heights of Bellevue
View of the Point of the Island of Bas-Meudon
View of the Quai de l'Arsenal
View of Parc Montsouris

1896

Twelfth Salon: April 1–May 31. Palais des Arts Libéraux, Champ-de-Mars.

Ten paintings exhibited:

Portrait of Mme M.
A Philosopher
Portrait of Children
Portrait of Mlle M.
View of the Charenton Canal (Sunset)
View of Dahomey (Quai d'Alfortville)
View from the Heights of Bellevue
View of the Fortifications (Boulevard Gouvion-Saint-Cyr)
View of the Bois de Boulogne
View of the Pont de Sèvres and Saint-Cloud

1897

Thirteenth Salon: April 3–May 31. Palais des Arts Libéraux, Champ-de-Mars.

Nine paintings exhibited:

The Sleeping Gypsy
Portrait of M. and Mme E. F.
Portrait of Mlle V. B.
Portrait of Children
View of the Railroad Bridge from Lyon to Charenton
View of the Quai de Seine at Alfortville and the Pont d'Ivry
View of the Chair Factory and the Quai de Seine at Alfortville
Bouquet of Wild Flowers
Portrait of Mlle M.

1898

Fourteenth Salon: April 19–June 12. Palais de Glace, Champs-Elysées.

Five paintings exhibited:

The Fight for Life
View of the Rue Louis-Blanc at Alfortville
View of the Bois de Boulogne (Autumn)
View of the Banks of the Marne (Summer)
Portrait

1901

Seventeenth Salon: April 20–May 21. Grandes Serres de l'Exposition Universelle, Cours-la-Reine.

Seven paintings exhibited:

Unpleasant Surprise
In the Spring
Portrait of M. M.
Road to the Fort de Vincennes
Lake Daumesnil (Stormy effect)
Lake Daumesnil (Sunset)
View of the Bois de Vincennes as Seen on the Right of the Road to Paris

1902

Eighteenth Salon: March 29–May 5. Grandes Serres de l'Exposition Universelle, Cours-la-Reine.

Nine paintings and several drawings exhibited:

Happy Quartet
Portrait of a Child
Portrait of Mlle L.
View of the Pont d'Asnières (Sunset)
View of the Quai d'Asnières
View from Alfortville
A Spot in Bellevue
An Area of the Quai de Saint-Cloud
Vase of Flowers

1903

Nineteenth Salon: March 20–April 25. Grandes Serres of the City of Paris, Cours-la-Reine.

Eight paintings exhibited:

Lonely Spot

Baby's Party
View of Paris from the Quai d'Alfortville (Sunset)
Vase of Flowers
Banks of the Marne (Nogent)
Banks of the Marne (Charenton)
View of the Bois de Boulogne
An Area of the Quai d' Ivry

1904

Twentieth Salon: February 21–March 24. Grandes Serres of the City of Paris, Cours-la-Reine.

Four paintings exhibited:

Scouts Attacked by a Tiger
Portrait of a Young Girl
Portrait of a Child
Flowers

1905

Twenty-first Salon: March 24–April 30. Grandes Serres of the City of Paris, Cours-la-Reine.

Four paintings exhibited:

Country Wedding
Portrait of M. G.
Portrait of M. C.
Avenue de Breteuil

1906

Twenty-second Salon: March 20–April 30. Grandes Serres of the City of Paris, Cours-la-Reine.

Five paintings exhibited:

Liberty Inviting the Artists to Exhibit at the 22nd Salon des Indépendants
View of the Banks of the Oise
Portrait of M. F.
Portrait of M. Steven
Portrait of Mme Steven

1907

Twenty-third Salon: March 20–April 30. Serres du Cours-la-Reine.

Six paintings exhibited:

Representatives of Foreign Powers Come to Salute the Republic as a Peaceful Gesture
The Little Cherry Pickers (owned by M. C.)
Philosophical Thought (owned by M. R.)
Landscape, Banks of the Marne (owned by M. B.)
Breton Scene (owned by M. B.)
View of Alfortville (owned by M. B.)

1908

Twenty-fourth Salon: March 20–May 2. Serres du Cours-la-Reine.

Four paintings exhibited:

The Jungle: Tiger Attacking a Buffalo
The Football Players
Portrait of a Child

Landscape (owned by Mlle Vel.)

1909

Twenty-fifth Salon: March 25–May 2. Tuilerie Gardens (Serres de l'Orangerie).

Two paintings exhibited:

The Muse Inspiring the Poet
Portrait (Landscape) (owned by M. B.)

1910

Twenty-sixth Salon: March 18–May 1. Cours-la-Reine, Pont des Invalides.

One painting exhibited:

The Dream

Works Exhibited at the Salon d'Automne
1905–1907

1905

Third Salon: October 18–November 25. Grand Palais des Champs-Elysées.

Three paintings exhibited:

Hungry Lion
Landscape: Banks of the Oise (Champoval region)
Landscape: Banks of the Oise (Villa Mathilde, Champoval region)

1906

Fourth Salon: October 6–November 15. Grand Palais des Champs-Elysées.

One painting exhibited:

Merry Jesters

1907

Fifth Salon: October 1–22. Grand Palais des Champs-Elysées.

Four paintings exhibited:

The Snake Charmer (owned by M. D.)
Landscape, Outskirts of Asnières
Tropical Landscape
Tropical Landscape

315

Exhibitions

1886–1910

Salon des Indépendants (with the exception of 1899 and 1900)

1894

Probably exhibited studies in a group showing at the gallery "Chez le Barc de Boutteville," rue Le Peletier, Paris

1905–1907

Salon d'Automne

1909

Private exhibition, organized by Wilhelm Uhde, at a furniture store, rue Notre-Dame-des-Champs, Paris

After Rousseau's death

1910

November 18–December 8: Exhibition of paintings and drawings in the collection of Max Weber at the Alfred Stieglitz Gallery, New York. Organized by Max Weber

1911

April 20–June 13: Salle Rousseau at the 29th Salon des Indépendants. Retrospective exhibition

1912

October 28–November 9: Galerie Bernheim-Jeune, Paris.
27 paintings, 2 drawings.
Foreword to the exhibition by Wilhelm Uhde

1913

Salle Rousseau at the first German Salon d'Automne, Berlin

1923

June: Galerie Paul Rosenberg, Paris

1925

June: Grande Maison de Blanc, Paris

1926

March: Galerie Flechtheim, Berlin.
32 paintings.
Foreword to the exhibition by Wilhelm Uhde

1927

October: Lefèvre Gallery, London.
Foreword to the exhibition by Roch Grey

1931

January 2–February 12: Marie Harriman Gallery, New York.
31 paintings

February 20–March 1: Arts Club, Chicago.
7 paintings

1933

March 1–April 2: Kunsthalle, Basel.
56 paintings, 8 drawings

1937

March 3–31: Galerie Paul Rosenberg, Paris.
22 paintings

1942

January 22–February 23: Art Institute of Chicago.
43 paintings

March 18–May 3: Museum of Modern Art, New York.
42 paintings

1944

December 22–January 21, 1945: Musée d'Art Moderne, Paris.
21 paintings.
Foreword to the exhibition by Paul Eluard and A. Jakovsky

1945

March 2–April 2: Salle Rousseau at the 56th Salon des Indépendants. Retrospective exhibition

1950

Salle Rousseau at the XXVth Venice Biennale. Retrospective exhibition

1951

November 5–December 22: Sidney Janis Gallery, New York.
Foreword to the exhibition by Tristan Tzara

1961

February 10–April 16: Galerie Charpentier, Paris.
80 paintings

1963

April 17–May 25: Wildenstein Gallery, New York. Loan exhibition.
62 paintings.
Foreword to the exhibition by Maximilien Gauthier

Chronology

1844

Henri Julien Félix Rousseau born at Laval (Mayenne) May 21. Son of Julien Rousseau, tinsmith, and Eléonore, née Guyard, natives of Laval. He was their fourth child. There were three older sisters and a younger brother, Jules.

1832—Birth of Manet.
1839—Birth of Cézanne.
1840—Birth of Monet.
1841—Birth of Renoir.
1848—Birth of Gauguin.
1853—Birth of Van Gogh.
1859—Birth of Seurat.

1850

Student at the Lycée of Laval, where he seems to have remained until 1860.

1851

The family home is sold at auction to pay off the father's debts. The family moves first to Avesnières, near Laval, where his father is a wine salesman, later to Couptrain, in the same region, where he goes into another business. Henri Rousseau continues at the Lycée of Laval as a boarding student.

1860

Prizes for drawing and singing at the Lycée of Laval.

1863

Works for a lawyer, Maître Fillon, in Angers. Sentenced to a month's imprisonment for petty larceny. Hoping to avoid scandal, volunteers for seven years in the army (full term of military service at this time). Assigned to 51st Infantry Regiment, stationed in Angers. The regiment supplies replacements for the expeditionary force in Mexico, but Rousseau is not one of these. He probably meets soldiers back from the adventure in April 1867, at Angers, and hears their stories.

1863—Manet exhibits *Le Déjeuner sur l'herbe* at the Salon des Refusés.

1868

His father dies. July 15 he leaves the army, having served four years, excused as sole support of his widowed mother.

1869

Marries Clémence Boitard, originally from Saint-Germain-en-Laye. They will have nine children, most of whom die in infancy. The young couple lives at 15 rue Rousselet, Paris. Clerical job with a bailiff, Maître Radez. Enters the Paris toll service as second-class clerk, a rank he will never rise above, though posterity will assign him the rank of Douanier.

1870

Called up for two months' military service as private, but sees no action.

1873—Birth of Alfred Jarry at Laval.
1874—First exhibition of the Impressionists: Monet, Renoir, Cézanne, Sisley, Pissarro, Guillaumin, Degas, Berthe Morisot.

1876

Birth of daughter Julia. She later becomes Madame Bernard, and dies in 1956. Her daughter, Jeanne Bernard, lives in Cherbourg where she gives piano lessons.

1880—Birth of Guillaume Apollinaire.
1881—Birth of Picasso.
1882—Birth of Braque.

1884

Granted permission to work as copyist in the national museums.

1884—Founding of the Salon des Indépendants, the first salon to dispense with jury and prizes.

1885

Two paintings reportedly sent to the Salon des Champs-Elysées: *Italian Dance* and *Sunset*.

1886

Exhibits for the first time at the Salon des Indépendants, as he will for the rest of his life, except for the years 1899 and 1900. Among the painters this year are Signac, and Seurat, who shows *Sunday Afternoon on the Island of La Grande Jatte*. Later, other exhibitors will be Toulouse-Lautrec, Van Gogh, Cézanne, Bonnard, and Matisse. Rousseau is living at 135 rue de Sèvres.

1888

His wife dies. His daughter Julia goes to live in Angers with the painter's brother.

1889

Paris World's Fair. Rousseau profoundly impressed, and his painting influenced. He writes a full-length comedy, *A Visit to the 1889 Fair*. He is living at 18–bis Impasse du Maine.

1889—Toulouse-Lautrec exhibits *Le Moulin de la Galette* at the Salon des Indépendants.

1890—Death of Van Gogh.

1891

Paints the portrait of Pierre Loti and exhibits first exotic work at the Salon des Indépendants: *Surprised! (Storm in the Forest)*.

1891—Gauguin leaves for Tahiti.
1891—Death of Seurat.

1892

Takes part in a painting competition held by the municipality of Paris and receives a silver medal.

1893

Retires from the Paris toll service and devotes himself wholly to painting. Meets Jarry. Is living at 44 avenue du Maine.

1893—Ambroise Vollard opens his gallery.

1894

Exhibits *War* at the Salon des Indépendants. The picture is lost, but turns up at Louviers during the Second World War, and is now in the Louvre. Very probably had an exhibition of studies at the gallery "Chez le Barc de Boutteville," rue Le Peletier.

1895

Exhibits the portrait of Alfred Jarry (since destroyed) at Salon des Indépendants. The magazine *L'Imagier*, edited by Rémy de

319

Gourmont, publishes a lithograph by Rousseau, a first version of *War*.

1896—Alfred Jarry publishes *Ubu-Roi*.

1897

Shows *The Sleeping Gypsy* at the Salon des Indépendants. Jarry shares his studio for a few weeks at 44 avenue du Maine.

1898

Writes the mayor of Laval offering to sell *The Sleeping Gypsy* for from 1,800 to 2,000 francs.

1899

September 2 marries Joséphine Noury, widow of M. Tensorer. Does not exhibit at the Indépendants. Writes a five-act play in collaboration with Mme Barkovsky and sends it to the Théâtre du Châtelet. Is living at 3 rue Vercingétorix.

1900

Does not exhibit at the Salon des Indépendants. Takes part in a painting competition at the town hall of Asnières. It is probably during this period that he plays in the orchestra of the Amicale of the Fifth Arrondissement, becomes a sales inspector for the newspaper *Le Petit Parisien* in his quarter, and begins to give music and painting lessons at home—an activity he continues to the end of his life.

1901

Exhibits *Unpleasant Surprise* at the Salon des Indépendants. Teaches drawing class at the Ecole Philotechnique, rue d'Alésia. Is living at 3 rue Gassendi.

1903

Second wife dies.

1903—Founding of the Salon d'Automne.

1904

Exhibits *Scouts Attacked by a Tiger* at the Salon des Indépendants. This is the first of his tropical landscapes. His waltz *Clémence* is published.

1905

At the Salon d'Automne, in the same hall with the Fauves, exhibits the *Hungry Lion*, a big canvas reproduced in *L'Illustration française*, November 4.

1906

Introduced by Jarry to Apollinaire. Also knows Robert Delaunay. Is living at 2-bis rue Perrel.

1907

At the Salon d'Automne exhibits *The Snake Charmer*, a painting commissioned by Delaunay's mother. At the Salon des Indépendants he exhibits *Representatives of Foreign Powers*. . . .On December 2 he is imprisoned for fraud. Released pending trial December 31.

1907—Picasso paints *Les Demoiselles d'Avignon*.

1908

Picasso arranges a tribute to Rousseau, an evening party at his studio in the Bateau-Lavoir. In his own studio in the Rue Perrel, Rousseau begins to hold his famous "musical and family evenings." The programs include music he has written.

1909

Tried on January 9, he is given a suspended sentence of two years and fined 100 francs. His paintings begin to sell. Vollard buys his pictures, as does the dealer Brummer, whose portrait he paints. Wilhelm Uhde arranges his first one-man show at a furniture shop in the Rue Notre-Dame-des-Champs. Roch Grey, Serge Férat, and Ardengo Soffici admire him and buy pictures. He exhibits the portrait of Apollinaire and Marie Laurencin, *The Muse Inspiring the Poet*, at the Salon des Indépendants, and a second version of the same. Falls in love with a fifty-four-year-old widow named Léonie, a saleswoman at the Economie ménagère, who rejects his advances.

1910

Exhibits *The Dream* at the Salon des Indépendants. Dies alone at the Hôpital Necker September 2. Buried September 4 at the Bagneux cemetery in a pauper's grave. The following year his friends Queval and Robert Delaunay obtain a thirty-year plot to which his remains are removed. In 1947 they are again removed, this time to the Parc de la Perrine at Laval.

Bibliography

AJALBERT, J. "La Leçon du Douanier," *Beaux Arts* (October 1, 1937)

ALEXANDRE, A. "Le Salon des Indépendants," *Comoedia* (April 3, 1909)

APOLLINAIRE, G. *Chroniques d'Art* (1902–1918), Paris, 1960

——. "Le Douanier," *Soirées de Paris* (January 15, 1914), No. 20, (through an error this issue of *Soirées de Paris* carries the date 1913)

ARAGON, L. "De Fouquet à Lefranc," *Arts de France*, No. 15–16, pp. 27–43

BASLER, A. *Henri Rousseau, sa vie, son œuvre*, Paris, 1927

——. "Le Douanier Rousseau," *L'Art vivant*, 1926, pp. 777–783

——. "M. Paul Guillaume et sa collection de tableaux," *L'Amour de l'Art*, 1929, pp. 253–256

——. "Recollections of Henri Rousseau," *The Arts*, 1927, pp. 313–319

BAZIN, G. "La Guerre du Douanier Rousseau," *Bulletin des Musées de France*, 1. XI, 1946, No. 2, pp. 8–9

BENDER, E. "Die XXIV. Ausstellung der Berliner Secession," *Deutsche Kunst und Dekoration* (August, 1912), pp. 283–294

BERNARD, J. "La petite fille de Rousseau raconte la vie de son grand-pére," *Arts* (October 17, 1947)

BONMARIAGE, S. "Apollinaire et Rousseau," *Partisans* (May, 1924), pp. 7–8

BOURGEOIS, S., and GEORGE, W. "L'art français de XIXe et XXe siècles à la collection Adolphe et Samuel Lewisohn," *Formes*, 1932, pp. 300–307

BRETON, A. *Le Surréalisme et la peinture*, New York, 1945

——. "Génèse et perspectives artistiques du Surréalisme," *Labyrinthe*, 1945, No. 5, pp. 10–11; No. 6, pp. 4–5

BUZZICHINI, M. *Henri Rousseau*, Milan, 1944

CARRÀ, C. "Rousseau le Douanier and the Italian Tradition," *Magazine of Art*, Vol. 44, 1941, pp. 261–267

CERTIGNY, H. *La Vérité sur le Douanier Rousseau*, Paris 1961

——. "La carrière militaire du Douanier Rousseau," *La Revue des deux mondes* (February 15, 1901), pp. 702–708

——. "Henri Rousseau, cet inconnu," *Les Nouvelles Litteraires* (February 9, 1961)

——. "Le Douanier Rousseau et l'Association Philotechnique," *Preuves*, No. 122, pp. 26–30

CHASSÉ, C. *Dans les coulisses de la gloire: d'Ubu-Roi au Douanier Rousseau*, Paris, 1947

——. "D'Ubu-Roi au Douanier Rousseau," *Grande Revue* (April, 1923)

——. "Les défenseurs des fausses gloires —les amis du Douanier Rousseau," *Grande Revue* (May, 1924)

CLARÉTIE, G. "Compte-rendu du procès de Rousseau," *Le Figaro* (January 10, 1909)

COGNIAT, R. "Figures de collectionneurs: Jacques Doucet," *Formes*, 1930, pp. 10–11

——. "La collection Marcel Monteux," *L'Amour de l'Art*, 1931, pp. 259–364

COOPER, D. *Rousseau*, Paris, 1951

——. "Le Douanier Rousseau," *The Burlington Magazine* (July, 1944)

COQUIOT, G. *Les Indépendants*, Paris, 1921

——. *Vagabondages à travers la peinture et les paysages, les bêtes et les hommes*, Paris, 1921

COURTHION, P. *Henri Rousseau, le Douanier*, Geneva, 1944

——. *Henri Rousseau*, Paris, 1956

——. "Der Urwald, Gemälde von Henri Rousseau," *Du*, 1949, No. 1, pp. 17–20

——. "Henri Rousseau," *L'Oeil* (October, 1958), No. 46, pp. 18–27

DÄUBLER, T. *Der Neue Standpunkt*, Dresden, 1957

DELAUNAY, R. "Henri Rousseau le Douanier," *L'Amour de l'Art* (November, 1920), pp. 228–230

——. "Mon ami Rousseau," *Les Lettres Françaises* (August 7, 1952), No. 369; (August 21, 1952), No. 370; (August 28, 1952), No. 371; (September 4, 1952), No. 372

DELAUNAY, S. "Documents retrouvés," *Labyrinthe*, 1946, No. 2, pp. 3–5

——. "Images inédites du Douanier Rousseau," *Les Lettres Françaises* (August 1, 1952), No. 368

DORMOY, M. "La collection Jacques Doucet," *Kunst und Künstler*, 1928–29, pp. 233–36

DREYFUS, A. "Henri Rousseau le Douanier," *Kunstchronik* (February, 1914), No. 20, col. 340–42

EBERLEIN, K. "Rousseau oder die Matrosenkunst," *Kunstchronik und Kunstmarkt*, 1926, pp. 721–24

EGGER, C. "Henri Rousseau, Ausstellung in der Basler Kunsthalle," *Die Kunst*, 1933, pp. 225–28

EINSTEIN, C. *Die Kunst des 20. Jahrhunderts*, Berlin, 1926

FELS, F. "En marge de l'exposition Rousseau à la Marie Harriman Gallery à New York," *Formes*, 1931, pp. 10–12

FIERENS, P. "Henri Rousseau," *Journal des Débats* (June 21, 1927)

FORTINI, F. *Henri Rousseau le Douanier*, Ivrea, n. d.

FOURNIER, G. "Henri Rousseau à l'auberge de 'La Faisane,'" *Les Lettres Françaises* (September 11, 1952), No. 373

FRANCIS, H. S. "The Jungle by Henri-Julien Rousseau," *Bulletin of the Cleveland Museum of Art*, Vol. 36, 1949, pp. 170–78

GARÇON, M. *Le Douanier Rousseau, accusé naïf*, Paris, 1953

GAUTHIER, M. *Le Douanier Rousseau*, Paris, 1949

——. *Henri Rousseau*, Paris, 1956

——. "La maison natale du Douanier," *Beaux-Arts* (December 3, 1937)

——. "Henri Rousseau," *Biennale de Venise*, 1950, No. 1, pp. 12–14

GEORGE, W. "La grande peinture contemporaine à la collection Paul Guillaume," *La Renaissance*, 1921, pp. 173–85

——. "La collection Fukushima," *La Renaissance*, 1930, pp. 102–3

——. "Le Miracle de Henri Rousseau," *Les Arts à Paris*, 1930, No. 18, pp. 3–11

GEORGES-MICHEL, M. *De Renoir à Picasso, Les peintres que j'ai connus*, Paris, 1954

GLASER, K. "Die XXIV Ausstellung Berliner Secession," *Die Kunst* (June, 1912), pp. 413–31

GRENIER, J. "Henri Rousseau" (the Rousseau Exhibition at the Galerie Charpentier), *Preuves* (April, 1961), No. 122, pp. 59–60

GREY, R. *Henri Rousseau* (with an introduction by André Salmon), Paris, 1943

——. *Rousseau*, Rome, 1922

——. "Le Douanier Rousseau," *Action* (May 7, 1921)

——. "Souvenir de Rousseau," *Soirées de Paris* (January 15, 1914), No. 20

GRIMOD, J. "Lettre de Rousseau proposant *La Bohémienne Endormie* à sa ville natale," *Le Petit Journal* (January 7, 1935)

GRIOT, A. "The Centenary of Henri Rousseau," *Art Quarterly* VII, (Summer, 1944), No. 3, pp. 207–18

GUENNE, J. "La naïveté est-elle un art?" *L'Art vivant*, 1931, p. 140

HUYGHE, R. "La peinture d'instinct," *L'Amour de l'Art*, 1933, pp. 185–88

JACOMETTI, N. "Henri Rousseau, dit le Douanier," *Le Point*, 1937, No. 3, pp. 87–88

JAKOVSKY, A. *Les feux de Montparnasse*, Paris, 1957

——. *Les peintres naïfs*, Paris, 1956

JOHNSTONE, J.-H. "La collection Stoop à Londres," *L'Amour de l'Art*, 1932, pp. 197–202

JOURDAIN, F. "A propos de quelques peintres autodidactes," *Arts de France*, 1946, No. 2, pp. 9–16

KIESER, R. "Henri Rousseau" (the Rousseau exhibition at the Galerie Bernheim-Jeune), *Kunst und Künstler* (January, 1913), pp. 218–20

KOLLE, H. *Henri Rousseau*, Leipzig, 1922

————. "Henri Rousseau," *Der Cicerone* (July, 1921), pp. 371–84

KÜPPERS. "Die Sammlung Max Leon Flemming in Hamburg," *Der Cicerone* (January, 1922), pp. 3–15

LAPORTE, P. M. "Humanism and the Contemporary Primitive," *Gazette des Beaux-Arts*, Vol. 29, 1946, pp. 47–62

LE DIBERDER, Y. "Rousseau s'inspirait-il de photos de gravures?" *Arts*, Vol. 26, (December, 1947)

LE PICHON, Y. "Les sources de Rousseau révélées," *Arts* (February 15, 1961)

————. "Le secret du Douanier Rousseau," *Elle* (February 10, 1961), No. 790

LO DUCA, J.-M. *Henri Rousseau, dit le Douanier*, Paris, 1951

LOTHE, A. *Parlons peinture, essais*, Paris, 1936

————. "Henri Rousseau" (the Rousseau exhibition at the Paul Rosenberg Gallery), *La Nouvelle Revue Française* (November 1, 1923)

————. "L'Art Populaire," *La Nouvelle Revue Française* (August 1, 1929)

MARINI, R. "Il problema di Rousseau le Douanier," *Emporium*, Vol. 114, 1951, pp. 79–83

MILLE, P. "Le peintre Henri Rousseau," *Le Temps* (January 28, 1913)

MILLIKEN, W. M. "A painting by Papa Rousseau," *Bulletin of the Cleveland Museum of Art*, 1930, pp. 8–10

MÖBIUS, R. "Henri Rousseau, zum Selbstbildnis von 1890," *Der Cicerone*, 1926, No. 6, p. 179

NEBBIA, U. "Sul movimento pittorico contemporaneo," *Emporium* (December, 1913), pp. 412–38

OLIVIER, F. *Picasso et ses amis*, Paris, 1933

PERRUCHOT, H. *Le Douanier Rousseau*, Paris, 1957

PIEXOTTO, M. "The Lewisohn Collection," *Studio* VII, 1939, pp. 95–107

PODESTÀ, A. "Henri Rousseau," *Emporium*, Vol. 112, 1950, pp. 11–16

RAGGHIANTI, C. "I Primitivi," *Sele-Arte*, 1955, No. 16, pp. 2–5

RAYNAL, M. "Le banquet Rousseau," *Soirées de Paris* (January 15, 1914), No. 20

REWALD, J. "French Paintings in the Collection of Mr. and Mrs. John Hay Whitney," *The Connoisseur*, Vol. 137, 1956, pp. 134–40

RICH, D. C. *Henri Rousseau*, New York, 1946

ROGER-MARX, C. "Le couple," *Formes et couleurs*, 1946, No. 2, pp. 29–38

ROH, F. "Ein neuer Henri Rousseau" (concerning *The Sleeping Gypsy*), *Jahrbuch der Jungen Kunst*, 1924, pp. 57–60

————. "Henri Rousseau, Bildform und Bedeutung für die Gegenwart, *Die Kunst*, Vol. 27, 1927, pp. 105–14

SALMON, A. *Henri Rousseau, dit le Douanier*, Paris, 1927

————. "Henri Rousseau," *Revue de France* (August 1, 1922)

————. "Un peintre naïf. Le souvenir du Douanier," *Jardin des Arts*, 1955, No. 6, pp. 376–82

SCHWARZ, H. "Art and Photography: Forerunners and Influences," *Magazine of Art*, Vol. 42, 1949, pp. 252–57

SHATTUCK, R. *The Banquet Years. The Arts in France: 1885–1918*, London, 1959

SOFFICI, A. "Henri Rousseau," *La Voce* (September 15, 1910), No. 40

SOUPAULT, P. *Henri Rousseau*, Paris, 1927

————. *Henri Rousseau, Le Douanier*, Geneva, 1948

————. "Henri Rousseau," *Feuilles libres* (August-September, 1922)

————. "La légende du Douanier Rousseau," *L'Amour de l'Art*, 1926, pp. 333–37

STEIN, G. *L'autobiographie d'Alice Toklas*, Paris, 1934

SZITTYA, E. *Malerschicksale: Vierzehn Porträts*, Hamburg, 1925

TERRIER, M. "Le portrait du Douanier Rousseau par Robert Delaunay au Musée de Laval," *Musées de France*, 1949, pp. 103–4

TROHEL, J. "Origines Mayennaises du Douanier Rousseau," *Mercure de France* (August 1, 1928), pp. 710 ff.

————. "Alfred Jarry et les huissiers," *Mercure de France* (May 1, 1934)

TZARA, T. *Henri Rousseau*, Zurich, 1958
————. Preface to *Une visite à l'Exposition de 1889* by Henri Rousseau, Geneva, 1947

UHDE, W. *Henri Rousseau*, Paris, 1911
————. *Henri Rousseau*, Düsseldorf, 1913
————. *Henri Rousseau*, Berlin, 1923
————. *Rousseau, le Douanier*, Bern, 1948
————. *Cinq maîtres primitifs* (preface by H. Bing-Bodmer), Paris, 1949
————. "Henri Rousseau," *Deutsche Kunst und Dekoration* (October-November, 1920), pp. 17–25
————. "Rousseau et les primitifs modernes," *L'Amour de l'Art*, 1933, pp. 189–96

VAUXCELLES, L. "Henri Rousseau," *Gil Blas* (September 7, 1910)
VOLLARD, A. *Souvenirs d'un marchand de tableaux*, Paris, 1948

WARNOD, A. *Les berceaux de la jeune peinture: Montmartre, Montparnasse*, Paris, 1925
WEBER, M. "Rousseau as I Knew Him," *Art News* (February 15, 1942)
WEHLE, H. B. "A Picture by Henri Rousseau," *Bulletin of the Metropolitan Museum of Art* XXXIV, 1939, p. 65
————. "The De Groot Collection," *Bulletin of the Metropolitan Museum of Art* V, 1947–48, pp. 264–71
WILENSKI, R. H. *Modern French Painters*, London, 1945
F. W. "Cleveland Museum's French Exhibition," *The Arts*, 1929–30, pp. 321–35

ZAHAR, M. "La peinture naïve," *L'Arche*, 1945, No. 11, pp. 123–29
————. "Le Douanier Rousseau" (Rousseau exhibition at the Musée d'Art Moderne, Paris), *L'Arche*, 1944–45, No. 7, pp. 112–13
ZERVOS, C. *Henri Rousseau*, Paris, 1927

Index of Names